THE VIETNAMESE

Other books in the
Coming to America series:

COMING TO AMERICA

THE VIETNAMESE

Michelle E. Houle, *Book Editor*

Bruce Glassman, *Vice President*
Bonnie Szumski, *Publisher*
Helen Cothran, *Managing Editor*

GREENHAVEN PRESS
An imprint of Thomson Gale, a part of The Thomson Corporation

THOMSON
™
GALE

Detroit • New York • San Francisco • San Diego • New Haven, Conn.
Waterville, Maine • London • Munich

© 2006 Thomson Gale, a part of The Thomson Corporation.

Thomson and Star Logo are trademarks and Gale and Greenhaven Press are registered trademarks used herein under license.

For more information, contact
Greenhaven Press
27500 Drake Rd.
Farmington Hills, MI 48331-3535
Or you can visit our Internet site at http://www.gale.com

Cover credit: © Tony Freeman/PhotoEdit

LIBRARY OF CONGRESS CATALOGING-IN-PUBLICATION DATA

The Vietnamese / Michelle E. Houle, book editor.
   p. cm. — (Coming to America)
Includes bibliographical references and index.
ISBN 0-7377-2769-1 (lib. : alk. paper)
   1. Vietnamese Americans—History. 2. Vietnamese Americans—Social conditions. 3. Immigrants—United States—History. 4. Refugees—United States—History. 5. Vietnam—Emigration and immigration—History. 6. United States—Emigration and immigration—History. 7. Vietnamese Americans—Biography. I. Houle, Michelle E. II. Coming to America (San Diego, Calif.)
E184.V53V537 2006
973'.049592—dc22
                                                            2005046131

Printed in the United States of America

CONTENTS

Chapter 1: Leaving Vietnam

   The formal unification of South and North Vietnam into
   the Socialist Republic of Vietnam in 1976 resulted in the
   imposition of communism on those who had just recently
   enjoyed democracy in South Vietnam. The unification
   fueled the exodus of hundreds of thousands of refugees.

   Seven years old when he fled Vietnam, Vu Tran describes
   the ordeal his family members experienced during their
   escape from Saigon via American military helicopters. He
   and many other Vietnamese left the country when Communists from North Vietnam took control of Saigon.

   A young girl describes her harrowing boat escape from
   Vietnam in 1979. As one of the "boat people," Tran Thi
   My Ngoc experienced many physical and mental tor-
   ments on her way to a better life in the United States.

Chapter 2: The First Waves of Immigrants Adapt to Their New Home

   After the Vietnam War, American refugee camps took in
   thousands of immigrants. The camps helped teach the

Chapter 3: Later Waves Up to the Present Day

Chapter 4: Accomplished Vietnamese Americans

FOREWORD

In her popular novels, such as *The Joy Luck Club* and *The Bonesetter's Daughter*, Chinese American author Amy Tan explores the complicated cultural and social differences between Chinese-born mothers and their American-born daughters. For example, the mothers eat foods and hold religious beliefs that their daughters either abhor or abstain from, while the daughters pursue educational and career opportunities that were not available to the previous generation. Generation gaps occur in almost all families, but as Tan's writings show, such differences are even more pronounced when parents grow up in a different country. When immigrants come to the United States, their initial goal is often to start a new life that is an improvement from the life they experienced in their homeland. However, while these newcomers may intend to fully adapt to American culture, they inevitably bring native customs with them. Immigrants have helped make America broader culturally by introducing new religions, languages, foods, and different ways of looking at the world. Their children and subsequent generations, however, often seek to cast aside these traditions and instead more fully absorb mainstream American mores.

As Tan's writings suggest, the dissimilarities between immigrants and their children are manifested in several ways. Adults who come to the United States and do not learn English turn to their children, educated in the American school system, to serve as interpreters and translators. Children, seeing what their American-born schoolmates eat, reject the foods of their native land. Religion is another area where the generation gap is particularly pronounced. For example, the liturgy of Syrian Christian services had to be translated into English when most young Syrian Americans no longer knew how to speak Syriac. Numerous Jews, freed from the European ghettos they had lived in, wished to assimilate more fully into the surrounding culture and began to loosen the traditional dietary and ritual requirements under which they had grown up. Reformed Judaism, which began in Germany, thus found a strong foothold among young Jews born in America.

However, no generational experiences have been as significant as that between immigrant mothers and their daughters. Living in the United States has afforded girls and young women opportunities they likely would not have had in their homelands. The daughters of immigrants, in some cases, live entirely different lives than their mothers did in their native nations. Where an Arab mother may have only received a limited education, her American-raised daughter enjoys a full course of American public schooling, often continuing on to college and careers. A woman raised in India might have been placed in an arranged marriage, while her daughter will have the opportunity to date and choose a husband. Admittedly, not all families have been willing to give their daughters all these new freedoms, but these American-born girls are frequently more willing to declare their wishes.

The generation gap is only one aspect of the immigrant experience in the United States. Understanding immigrants' unique and shared experiences and their contributions to American life is an interesting way to study the many people who make up the American citizenry. Greenhaven Press's Coming to America series helps readers learn why more people have moved to the United States than to any other nation. Selections on the lives of immigrants once they have reached America, from their struggles to find employment to their experiences with discrimination and prejudice, help give students insights into stereotypes and cultural mores that continue to this day. Finally, profiles of prominent immigrants help the reader become aware of the many achievements of these people in fields ranging from science to politics to sports.

Each volume in the Coming to America series takes an extensive look into a particular immigrant population. The carefully selected primary and secondary sources provide both historical perspectives and firsthand insights into the immigrant experience. Combined with an in-depth introduction and a comprehensive chronology and bibliography, every book in the series is a valuable addition to the study of American history. With immigrants comprising nearly 12 percent of the U.S. population, and their children and grandchildren constantly adding to the population, the immigrant experience continues to evolve. Coming to America is consequently a beneficial tool for not only understanding America's past but also its future.

INTRODUCTION

In early February 2005, three Vietnamese artists arrived in Seattle, Washington, to attend a gallery exhibition of their work. The exhibit, titled Viet Nam Now, featured a collection of impressionistic and abstract paintings drawn from contemporary Vietnam. When Cu Cong Nguyen, Hoa Dang, and Hai Pham sat down to lunch in a Vietnamese restaurant in the Chinatown district of Seattle, they were "glared at and disparaged by [Vietnamese American] diners."[1] Vietnamese artists, who must be granted permission to tour the United States by the Communist government of Vietnam, are seen by many in the Vietnamese American community as supporters or friends of the Communist regime. Nearly thirty years after the fall of Saigon, perceived Communist sympathizers continue to face reprisals in Vietnamese American communities across the United States. But as new generations of Vietnamese Americans come of age, the issue of communism becomes more complex. Antipathy toward the Communist government in Vietnam is stronger among the older generation that experienced the loss of their homeland firsthand. This visceral threat of communism is a feeling completely alien to younger generations.

In 2003 Mai Lan, a twenty-year-old member of the Vietnamese Student Association at San Jose State University, summed up the disconnect like this: "The older generation, they went through the war. There's a lot of hatred toward communism. The younger Vietnamese, they don't care that much about communism. It's just more about over here now."[2]

Communism, the reason the Vietnamese fled Vietnam for America, continues to affect relationships within the Vietnamese American community and the community's relationship with its nation of origin. In fact, without communism, Vietnam never would have been divided, North Vietnam never would have invaded South Vietnam, the United States never would have been involved there, and the Vietnamese never would have come to America in such great numbers. To understand how communism came to be a force in Vietnam, it is necessary to begin with the French invasion of the country in the nineteenth century.

French Colonialism

In 1858 the French military seized control of the Vietnamese city of Danang, and by 1895 all of Vietnam, Laos, and Cambodia were under French rule. The French renamed the region Indochina and exploited both its people and its natural resources. The Vietnamese peasantry in particular suffered under French rule. As servants to their French masters, Vietnamese were forced to pay stiff taxes on goods such as salt and alcohol. They were also subject to a type of slave labor known as corvée.[3]

This exploitation of the poor by the wealthy sowed seeds of discontent. According to author Audrey Seah,

> To keep up the myth of the superiority of the colonial masters, Vietnamese were denied responsible positions. [Vietnamese] could hope for little more than menial work or work on railways as ticket collectors and engineers. Ironically, it was the introduction of French literature— the teachings of [philosophers Jean-Jacques] Rousseau and Voltaire, and [Nobel Prize–winning author] Anatole France—combined with extreme poverty that fired a popular revolution.[4]

These writers are often associated with helping to articulate democratic principles.

In 1930 Ho Chi Minh organized the Indochinese Communist Party to revolt against the French. Minh and his followers formed the League for the Independence of Vietnam in 1939. Minh formed a guerrilla army called the Viet Minh to fight the French, and the struggle for independence led to the French Indochina War (1946–1954).

Communist Takeover

In 1954 the Viet Minh defeated the French at the pivotal battle of Dien Bien Phu. On July 20, as a result of the Geneva Peace Accords, Vietnam was divided roughly along the seventeenth parallel to form a northern zone, under Communist leader Ho Chi Minh, and a southern, demo-

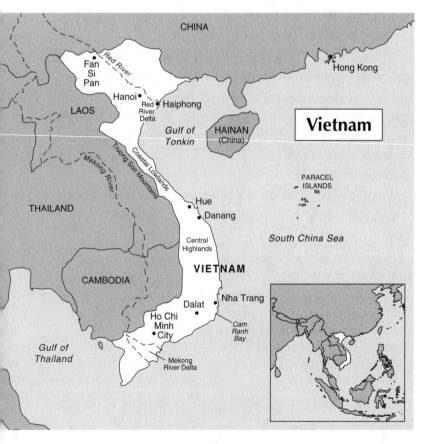

cratic zone, under Prime Minister Ngo Dinh Diem. North Vietnam declared itself an independent Communist nation, with a system of government derived from the teachings of Russian Communists Karl Marx and Vladimir Ilyich Lenin. According to the Vietnamese constitution, the Communist Party is the only force "leading the state and society." The totalitarian regime and the system of communism were anathema to Americans, who in the 1950s were in the midst of a Cold War against communism. Americans suspected of Communist sympathies were considered by many to be traitors and could be blackballed, or fired from their jobs. Americans felt that Communists were the country's greatest national threat. When North Vietnam began fighting against South Vietnam, trying to take over the country, Americans became deeply concerned about the situation.

Domino Theory

The United States, fearing an increase in Communist Power in Southeast Asia, supported the South Vietnamese in their struggle against Communist North Vietnam. One of the main motivations for U.S. involvement in Vietnamese affairs was a belief called the domino theory. This theory held that if a small nation like Vietnam could fall to communism, so might others. Historian Howard Zinn explains it this way:

> In the secret memoranda of the National Security Council (which advised the president on foreign policy) there was talk in 1950 of what came to be known as the "domino theory"—that, like a row of dominos, if one country fell to Communism, the next one would do the same and so on. It was important therefore to keep the first one from falling.[5]

In 1964, after North Vietnamese forces sank a U.S. battleship in the Gulf of Tonkin, Congress under President

Lyndon Johnson passed the Gulf of Tonkin Resolution. This legislation, authorizing the bombing of North Vietnam, marked the first official involvement of the United States in the Vietnam War. The U.S. military escalated its involvement for the next four years. Then, in 1968, Communist forces launched the Tet [Vietnamese New Year] Offensive, a series of surprise attacks against the South Vietnamese that marked a turning point in the Vietnam War.

In his memoir, author Nguyen Ngoc Ngan describes his wife's Tet tragedy: "Tuyet Lan . . . had relatives among the more than two thousand civilians in the Northern city of Hue who were forced to dig shallow trenches, then were lined up in front of them and shot in cold blood."[6] Nguyen Ngoc Ngan and his family, who unsuccessfully tried to escape Vietnam before the Communist takeover, faced a chaotic and terrifying scene when the North Vietnamese took control. On April 30, 1975, he writes, "the North Vietnamese Army, with disarming cries of *hoa binh* ("peace"), swept triumphantly into Saigon."[7] The victory of the Communists terrified the South Vietnamese who had fought against the North for years. Fearing retaliation, many South Vietnamese fled the country.

Vietnamese Exodus

The first significant immigration of Vietnamese to the United States occurred immediately after the fall of Saigon. Many of these new immigrants were airlifted out of Saigon provided they could prove their allegiance to the United States through government documents or written testimonials from U.S. citizens. Thousands of people were evacuated by helicopter from the roof of the U.S. Embassy.

This first wave of refugees numbered approximately 130,000. They were largely educated, anti-Communist, and friendly to U.S. interests. To assist this first wave, Congress passed the Indochina Migration and Refugee Assistance Act, which established short-term programs for resettlement. For those left behind, the situation in Vietnam was grim.

As journalist R. Scott Moxley writes, "Despite the promise of a healing brotherhood when Saigon fell in April 1975, Minh's disciples instead tortured or killed untold numbers of South Vietnamese and erected a barbaric, corrupt government and economic system that prompted more than a million people to flee their homeland in horror."[8]

Vietnam was a country ravaged by war. The massive bombing of Vietnam had depleted many natural resources. In this largely agricultural economy, the risk of starvation and poverty was very real. But government oppression was the determining factor in most flights. Simply put, many Vietnamese chose to risk death rather than risk life under the Communists.

In search of better conditions, the Vietnamese fled to many different places. For many, the United States, their ally in the war, was the destination of choice. The route to the United States for most Vietnamese refugees was less than direct. Many moved through camps in Guam, Thailand, or the Philippines before landing in one of the four transitional camps opened on the U.S. mainland in 1975. Families shared military barracks or tents. These camps provided English lessons, job training, recreation, and assistance in reunifying families torn apart by the war. These services helped the residents adjust to American culture and begin the transformation from refugees into immigrants. This first wave of Vietnamese immigrants, mainly urbanized and educated, arrived between 1975 and 1977 and tended to adjust well to life in the United States.

In contrast, the second wave of refugees, who left after 1978, tended to be less educated people from rural areas. Without the skills of the first-wave immigrants, these Vietnamese Americans faced a different set of challenges. They also lacked the assistance of the transitional camps established for the first waves. The Vietnamese who left after 1978 are often represented by the plight of the boat people. These refugees streamed out of Vietnam in small, unsafe boats, fleeing the poverty and oppression that accompanied the Communist invasion of South Vietnam.

Desperate Vietnamese often paid monumental ransoms for their passage. Families pooled resources to send relatives ahead, hoping their success would facilitate passage for the others. There are countless horror stories told about the plight of escapees. Along the escape route through the South China Sea, passengers faced bad weather, overcrowding, starvation, and piracy. In addition, nearby countries such as Thailand, Indonesia, and Malaysia did not guarantee asylum, and many boats were denied entry. The plight of these refugees garnered world media attention.

Reception in the United States

Americans' response to the influx of Vietnamese into the United States was a mixture of empathy, hostility, and guilt. Americans felt a sense of responsibility due to their involvement in the Vietnam War. Many Americans also had a hatred of communism, which led them to feel the need to help the Vietnamese. On the other hand, fear that a concentration of refugees would drain the financial resources of the affected communities where they settled led many Americans to resent the newcomers. To alleviate these concerns, the U.S. government established refugee dispersion policies.

Refugees were distributed to nearly every part of the United States. Many Vietnamese who settled in California and Texas in the 1970s and 1980s found work in the fishing industry. In Texas some native fishermen complained that competition by Vietnamese threatened to destroy their businesses. In 1979 hostilities increased to the point of violence, including the death of a white fisherman in Seadrift, Texas, and the destruction of several Vietnamese vessels.

After the Vietnamese were resettled throughout the United States, many first-wave refugees undertook a second migration. Vietnamese refugees began to reassemble themselves in ethnic enclaves as a means to increase their collective strength and power. California became a popular destination, as evidenced by the vibrant Vietnamese American community of Little Saigon in Orange County. As historian Hien Duc Do points out, in "San Jose and Westminster, California; Falls Church, Virginia; Fort Worth and Dallas, Texas; Seattle; and Boston, . . . families

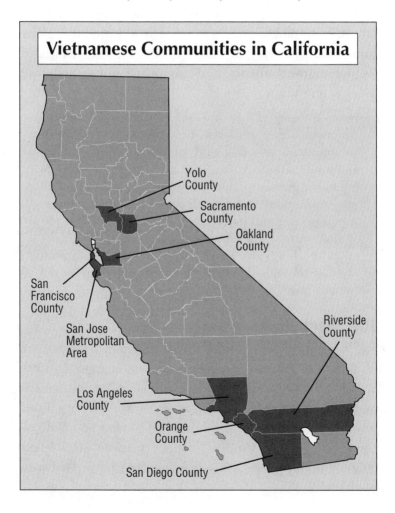

Vietnamese Communities in California

Yolo County

Sacramento County

Oakland County

San Francisco County

San Jose Metropolitan Area

Riverside County

Los Angeles County

Orange County

San Diego County

can be seen eating at any number of [Vietnamese] restaurants . . . [and] food found only in Asian or Vietnamese markets, including spices, fish sauce, certain vegetables, canned fruits from Asia, pickled vegetables, other sauces, and dried goods," is readily available.[9]

Today, despite the shared hatred of communism that originally united the Vietnamese in America, dissenting opinions about communism are emerging. In a 2004 editorial, Do added his name to a list of prominent Vietnamese American scholars who criticized the anti-Communist rhetoric dominating debates in Vietnamese American communities. In particular, these scholars objected to legislation enacted by the communities of Garden Grove and Westminister, California, declaring "Communist-free zones." They write,

> Non-Vietnamese-Americans, and even many Vietnamese-Americans, may think that the Vietnamese-American community is united behind such an act. This is not so. Many Vietnamese-Americans have no wish to continue the fight against communism, but are very reluctant to say so, since an extremist element in the Vietnamese-American community resorts to protests, shouting and even violence to quell any such disagreement. . . . Many of us have long started redefining our relationship with Vietnam through our work, travels, commerce and social connections.[10]

The HiTek Protest

Still, within the Vietnamese community today, allegations of being Communist-friendly are serious charges. In 1999 hundreds of protesters converged on the HiTek video store in Westminster, California, after owner Truong Tran posted a picture of Ho Chi Minh and the flag of Communist Vietnam in his window. Just the image of Minh is extremely divisive. As *Asian Week* journalist Janet Dang points out,

It was under [Minh's] leadership that the group of civilians chased away the French and helped regain [Vietnam's] independence in 1954. It was also under his leadership that a civil war ensued with South Vietnam, killing 58,000 Americans and 3 million Vietnamese—both North and South.[11]

By some accounts, as many as fifteen thousand people protested during the weeks that Tran, a self-proclaimed advocate of Ho Chi Minh, maintained his display. He was forced to move when the landlord refused to renew his lease. The controversy over the HiTek protest surfaced again in November 2004 when VAX (the *Vietnamese American Experience* television series) aired clips from this event in a half-hour show. After the episode aired, the MTV-style series, which appeals to a young adult Vietnamese American audience, was taken off the air.

The Younger Generation

But it is the younger generation that will determine the future path of the Vietnamese American community. Although young Vietnamese Americans understand why their parents left Vietnam and appreciate their interest in their home of origin, these youths are more focused on their lives in America. In 2004 journalist Rachel Tran asked a group of high school seniors what they thought was important to Vietnamese Americans today. Tran reports,

Thuy Linh Le . . . a Vietnamese-American junior at Central York High School . . . vows to give her children much more freedom than her parents give her now. Nonetheless, both she and [classmate Joanne] Nguyen are very determined to teach their children the Vietnamese language and their heritage. . . . Many young Vietnamese understand all of the hardships their parents had to overcome, but also, as Le says, they realize that "the whole point of coming [to the United States] was so the future generation wouldn't suffer as much.". . . When asked what is important for second-generation Vietnamese in the United States, Nguyen says, "Pretty much stepping up and showing your parents that you're capable of taking advantage of all that's provided here, and to show them that you can have that life that they always hoped for when they first came here."[12]

Why Communism Still Matters

In the year 2005, thirty years after the fall of Saigon, large numbers of Vietnamese still desire to immigrate to the United States, surprising some policy makers and immigration analysts. A steady stream of refugees has continued to apply for immigration papers for a variety of reasons. Families who were split apart during and after the war send loved ones to reunite with their stateside kin in hopes of a better life. Anti-Communist political prisoners continue to file appeals for safe passage.

Vietnamese-U.S. relations are improving, as evidenced by the normalization of diplomatic relations between the two nations in 1995. But as Moxley notes, "Only in recent years have the communists—desperate for international economic assistance—loosened their control, but that's too little, too late for most refugees."[13] The history of the relationship between the United States and Vietnam is a long and complex one, centered primarily on that great political force called communism. The Vietnamese who came to America were fleeing communism and their descendants today continue to be affected by it.

Notes

1. Tan Vinh, "Vietnamese Clash over Art," *Seattle Times*, February 18, 2005.
2. Quoted in Associated Press, "Vietnamese Activists Push for Old Flag," CNN.com, May 23, 2003.
3. A corvée is a mandatory tax payable in the form of hard labor.
4. Seah, *Cultures of the World*, p. 23.
5. Howard Zinn, *The Twentieth Century*. New York: HarperCollins, 1998, p. 216.

6. Nguyen Ngoc Ngan, *The Will of Heaven*. Toronto: Van Lang, 1982, p. 4.

7. Nguyen, *The Will of Heaven*, p. 5.

8. R. Scott Moxley, "Fresh Division Appears in Little Saigon," *Orange County Weekly*, May 30–June 5, 2003.

9. Hien Duc Do, *The Vietnamese Americans*. Westport, CT: Greenwood Press, 1999, p. 10.

10. Viet Thanh Nguyen, "Academics Take Stand Against Viet-Am Anti-Communist Obsession," *Azine, the Asian American Movement Ezine*, June 6, 2004. www.aamovement.net./viewpoints/obsession2.html. Viet Thanh Nguyen is an associate professor of English and Asian American studies at the University of Southern California. Scholars who signed the *Azine* statement are Hien Duc Do of San Jose State University, Hung Thai of UC Santa Barbara, Jeffrey Brody of Cal State-Fullerton, Van Bich Thi Tran of the Social Science Research Council in New York, Nguyen-vo Thu-huong of UCLA, Yen Le Espiritu of UC San Diego, Phuong Nguyen of USC, and Dan Duffy of the University of North Carolina.

11. Janet Dang, "Ho Chi Minh Haters," *Asian Week*, March 30, 2000.

12. Rachel Tran, "The Next Step: Vietnamese-American Teens Build on Parent's Dreams," *York (PA) Daily Record*, February 3, 2004.

13. Moxley, "Fresh Division Appears in Little Saigon."

CHAPTER 1

Leaving Vietnam

COMING TO AMERICA

Why the Vietnamese Came to America

Ronald Takaki

The country of Vietnam was divided along the seventeenth parallel on July 21, 1954, forming a northern zone, under Communist leader Ho Chi Minh, and a southern democratic zone under President Ngo Dinh Diem. North Vietnam declared itself an independent Communist nation, known as the Democratic Republic of Vietnam. The United States, fearing an increase in Communist power in Southeast Asia, reacted by supporting the South Vietnamese. In 1964 President Lyndon Johnson, suspecting North Vietnamese forces of sinking U.S. battleships in the Gulf of Tonkin, authorized the bombing of North Vietnam. Despite years of military involvement by the United States, however, on April 30, 1975, North Vietnamese Communist forces seized control of South Vietnam.

In the following selection Ronald Takaki describes the ensuing panic in South Vietnam. Fearing persecution from the Communists, hundreds of thousands of people left Vietnam in waves of departures that lasted throughout the last half of the twentieth century. With the fall of Saigon, many Vietnamese were airlifted out of the city by U.S. military personnel. Further waves escaped by boat. The extraordinary numbers of people who fled by boat faced innumerable threats, from drowning in turbulent seas to being attacked by pirates. Those fortunate enough to escape these calamities were often refused entry into neighboring countries, which were concerned about the effects that nearly a million refugees would have on their nations. By 1985, according to Takaki, 643,200 Vietnamese lived in the United States.

Ronald Takaki, *Strangers from a Different Shore: A History of Asian Americans.* Boston: Little, Brown and Company, 1989. Copyright © 1989 by Ronald Takaki. All rights reserved. Reproduced by permission of the publisher.

In 1964 there were only 603 Vietnamese living in the United States. They were students, language teachers, and diplomats. They were from South Vietnam, a country that had begun to receive increasing attention in the news. Vietnam had been a French colony since the late nineteenth century; beginning in World War II, the Vietminh, under the leadership of Ho Chi Minh, fought the French to regain their country's independence. This war culminated in 1954 when the French forces were defeated at the battle of Dien Bien Phu. At Geneva shortly afterward, the French and Vietminh signed an agreement that provided for a temporary partition of Vietnam at the seventeenth parallel and for an all-Vietnamese election in 1956. But a year after the Geneva conference, a new government was formed in the south headed by Ngo Dinh Diem, with the support of the United States, to counter the government in the north backed by China and the Soviet Union. The partition of Vietnam became permanent: the election was never held and civil war erupted. United States involvement in the conflict began to expand significantly in the early sixties when President John Kennedy sent Special Forces to Vietnam and when President Lyndon Johnson asked Congress to give him war powers in the 1964 Gulf of Tonkin Resolution. The war ended disastrously for South Vietnam and the United States eleven years later, precipitating a massive exodus of Vietnamese to the United States.

Unlike the other Asian groups already in America, the 1975 wave of Vietnamese migrants did not choose to come here. In fact, they had no decision to make, for they were driven out by the powerful events surrounding them. Most of them were military personnel and their families, in flight from the North Vietnamese troops. A week before the collapse of the South Vietnamese government on April 29, ten to fifteen thousand people were evacuated; then in a frenzy during the last days of April, 86,000 Vietnamese were airlifted out of the besieged country. "That morning, April 29," former Premier Nguyen Cao Ky recalled, describing his last hours in Saigon, "I found myself alone at the big headquarters of the general staff. . . . At noontime, all the American helicopters came in for the final, big evacuation. On the ground, there were hundreds of thousands of Vietnamese, running—right, left, every way, to find a way to escape. My bodyguards said to me, 'Well, General, it's time for us to go, too.'"

Chaos in the Streets

At street level, panic gripped the people. "On those last days of April," remembered a refugee, "[there was] a lot of gunfire and bombing around the capital. People were running on chaotic streets. We got scared. . . . We went to an American building where a lot of Americans and their Vietnamese associates were ready to be picked up by American helicopters." They could "feel" the bombing. "Our houses were shaking," said Thai Dang. "Then afterwards we went outside and saw abandoned guns and army uniforms on the streets. The soldiers in flight had thrown away their weapons and taken off their clothes. Here and there we saw bodies."

The city shuddered under relentless missile bombardments; homes and buildings were burning everywhere.

> Fires spring up like dragon's teeth
> At the standpoints of the universe:
> A furious, acrid wind sweeps them toward us from all
>   sides. . . .
> All around, the horizon burns with the color of death.

In a frenzy, frightened people rushed to get out of Saigon. From the roof of the American embassy, hundreds climbed frantically onto helicopters. Others drove to the airport, where they abandoned their cars with notes on the windshields: "For those who are left behind." Terrifying images had been seared into the minds of the refugees. "What was the one event during the trip [evacuation] you will never forget?" an interviewer asked a Vietnamese woman en route from the Philippines to the United States. "It was when all of these people were trying to get on the plane at the airport," she replied. "I saw people jamming the door and women and children could not get on. The shelling came closer and then the plane took off with people still hanging at the door."

Others left by boat. "There was a lot of bombing during the night and the next morning people were rushing to the barges," said Linh Do. "My mother was carrying my two-year-old sister wrapped in a blanket. She had lost her shoes and was running barefoot." Another Vietnamese girl recalled how she and her family scrambled to board a small boat with fifty other people. "I could hear the noisy firing guns, screams from injured people on the beach, and cries of little children," she wrote later. "While standing on the boat, I couldn't think of anything. It was not until sunset, when it was dark, that I stopped staring back and started worrying about the waves. It rained all night. I was all wet and cold. Holding each other, my brother and I prayed. The next day at noon time, we reached an American ship. As soon as the ship lowered one of its stairs, everybody climbed up the stairs without any order. Men, women and children were pushed aside and dropped into the sea. Some were crushed between boats. I carried my youngest brother and went up that stairs with fear." During the next few weeks, forty to sixty thousand Vietnamese escaped in boats to the open sea, where they were picked up by American navy ships and transported to Guam and the Philippines.

No Time to Prepare

The refugees had no time to prepare psychologically for departure; more than half of the refugees later said they were given less than ten hours. "I was afraid of the killings when the Communists came to town," one of them explained, expressing the concern of most refugees. Some did not even know for certain who would be going and who would be staying: "Mother came along to the airport. Then at the last minute she stayed behind because the number of children staying was larger than those leaving." Others thought they would be gone for only a month or two: "My mother would never have left her other six children behind if she thought she wasn't coming back." Many did not even know they were leaving or where they were going. "I saw everyone running to the harbor, so I decided to go along," recalled a Vietnamese. After reaching the Philippines, a family learned they were bound for the United States; later they said: "We did not plan on taking this trip."

Altogether some 130,000 Vietnamese refugees found sanctuary in the United States in 1975. The first-wave refugees generally came from the educated classes: 37 percent of the heads of households had completed high school and 16 percent had been to college. Almost two thirds could speak English well or with some fluency. Generally, the refugees came from the urban areas, especially Saigon; they were more westernized than the general population. They had worked with the French and then the Americans. About half of them were Christian, a group representing only 10 percent of the people in Vietnam. They came as family units rather than as young single men; almost half were female. After their arrival in the United States, the 1975 refugees were initially placed in processing camps like Pendleton in California and Fort Chaffee in Arkansas. From the camps they were spread throughout the country but they soon began to gather in communities such as Orange County, California.

Meanwhile, in Vietnam the fighting had stopped and "everything had fallen into absolute silence, a silence that was so unusual." Then the new Communist government began the reconstruction of society. Businesses were nationalized and reeducation camps were instituted for individuals associated with the old regime. "New Economic Zones" were developed for the movement of the population to the countryside. Thousands of Vietnamese, particularly urban business and professional elites, were ordered to "go to the country to do labour, the hard jobs, to make the irrigation canals, sometimes for one month, sometimes for two, or three months." "I remember the choked mute lines of families trudging out of the cities to begin agricultural work in the countryside," said an ethnic-Chinese businessman. "They had no prior knowledge of how to do that job, yet they had no choice." One of them said: "Life was very hard for everybody. All had changed! . . . I could see no future for me in Vietnam, no better life! I wanted to escape."

Risking Their Lives

Thousands did escape—21,000 in 1977, 106,500 in 1978, over 150,000 in 1979, and scores of thousands more later. The second-wave Vietnamese refugees took their wives and children and boarded crowded, leaky boats, risking their lives at sea where storms threatened to drown them and pirates waited to rob them and rape the women. Two thirds of the boats were attacked by pirates, each boat an average of more than two times.

> *Can you imagine human hair*
> *Flowing all over the sea,*
> *Children's bodies ready to dissolve*
> *As human meat dinners of fish?*
>
> *But they keep on leaving*
> *As humanity turn their heads away*
> *And still they serenely*
> *Throw themselves into death.*

Thai Dang remembered how she left on February 19, 1981, when she was only thirteen years old. "I just wanted to embrace my dear friend, Trang, tightly, telling her that I would be leaving Saigon in an hour, that she would always remain my friend." But she had to keep her planned escape a secret. "So, I left briefly, as if chased by a ghost, before they could see my eyes getting red. . . . I was yearning to capture each familiar scene, each beloved face of the place I had lived and grown up." But as Dang and other refugees were on their way to the hiding place of the boat, they were "discovered and hunted like beasts" by the Vietnamese forces. "I ran, fell, and ran for my life in the unknown darkness of a strange forest, totally oblivious to my bleeding wounds." Her mother placed her on a small boat and waved good-bye, and Dang wondered: "Who was to guarantee that I would survive in the dark sea?" But at sea they were attacked by Thai pirates. "The pirates, wearing almost nothing but frightening tattoos, jumped into our boat with axes and guns to rob and beat us. The air was saturated with the most disheartening cries. . . . We were literally begging on our knees."

Luong Bot Chau told a similar story. She and her husband, along with over two dozen refugees, had sailed away on a small, thirty-foot vessel. Off the coast of Thailand, their boat was attacked by Thai pirates. The pirates chopped off one of her husband's fingers to get his ring and then tried to slit his throat. "But the knife they had was too blunt," she said later. Instead they clubbed him to death and threw his body into the sea. Then they dragged the young girls up to the deck and systematically raped them. "We heard them scream and scream," Luong Bot Chau cried. "We could not get out, because the pirates had nailed down the hatch." Thirty-six-year-old Hue, who now lives in Sunnyvale, California, vividly remembered what happened to her on a boat in the Gulf of Thailand. When they saw the Thai pirates approaching their boat, Hue and the other women smeared their faces with engine oil and fish sauce to diminish their appeal. But the pirates ordered them to bathe and then raped them. Hue still wakes up screaming from nightmares of the experience—the "dark skinned men" encircling her, the knife at her throat, the hands that "clawed," and the teeth that "bit," mutilating her breasts. Two other women survivors recounted the horror they experienced: "The pirates tied them [the Vietnamese men] up and threw them into the water. The remaining people were tied up too, and locked in the hold after being stripped of their belongings. After this, the pirates came . . . to pillage and rape people. One person was killed after being dealt a blow with an iron bar. Another had his finger cut off because he was unable to pull off his wedding ring. When everything was looted, the pirates hurried to go. They released the men they kept in the hold and kicked them back to our boat. Some fell into the water and drowned with their hands bound behind their backs."

The survivors floated to Thailand, where they were forced to live in squalid refugee camps for months (and in the case of many individuals, for years). From the camps they went to countries like Australia, Canada, and France. Most of them came to the United States. "In 1978 my sister, Nguyet, my brothers Tinh, Hung, my father, and I left the country," wrote Tuyet Ahn Nguyen in a letter to me. "My mom and sister and couple of brothers stayed in Vietnam. It was so hard for my family to suffer the separation." The second-wave refugees were diverse, including educated professionals as well as fishermen, farmers, and storekeepers from the rural areas and small coastal cities and villages. Unlike the earlier refugees from Saigon, most of them did not speak English. Approximately 40 percent of the second wave were ethnic-Chinese Vietnamese. They had experienced hostility from Vietnamese society for decades, and became targets for discrimination under the new Communist regime. The government's program of nationalizing the economy focused heavily on the ethnic Chinese. Constituting 7 percent of the country's population, they controlled about 80 percent of its retail trade. Furthermore, military conflict had broken out between China and Vietnam in 1979, and the ethnic Chinese in Vietnam found themselves caught in the political crossfire.

In 1985 there were 643,200 Vietnamese in the United States. "Remember these are the people who were on our side," an American veteran of the Vietnam War said. "They have a right to come to this country as refugees. They just need a home."

Airlifted Out of Saigon

Vu Tran

On April 30, 1975, the North Vietnamese Communist army took control of Saigon in South Vietnam. Americans airlifted out Vietnamese fortunate enough to hold documents that could prove ties to American sponsors. In this article Vu Tran recounts his childhood escape from Vietnam at age seven. His mother had to make a wrenching decision to take him and his five younger brothers and sisters to America. Son of a South Vietnamese army military intelligence officer and a mother who was working for the CIA, Vu Tran was one of thousands evacuated by helicopter from the roof of the U.S. embassy. Vu Tran is currently an engineer in the aviation industry.

It was a dark and humid night with lots of thunder in the air. The thunder sound was not from a storm or from nature; it was from all the explosions that constantly haunted us. Ever since we received a letter from America a month earlier, everyone in the house was acting strange and secretive. The adults in the house whispered mostly and stopped talking when I or any other children were nearby.

But tonight was a different night; everyone was scurrying around the house packing their belongings into bags . . . it was mostly clothing and food. Mom also packed my clothes in bags and suitcases for me. I asked her what she and everyone else was doing, and Mom just told me to go look after my younger brothers and sisters. I'm the oldest of all the children. I was seven at the time.

After the packing was done, everyone waited for the sun to go down; and then we all headed to the bus station. I asked Mom where we were going, and Mom said "to visit grandma and grandpa." There were some people on the bus that Mom knew, and they asked Mom where's everyone going; and Mom replied that my grandpa died, and everyone is going to his funeral. I was shocked. . . . Mom never told me that grandpa died.

Several hours later, when we reached grandpa's house, he and grandma were sitting on his bed waiting for us. I looked at Mom and said, "Grandpa is still alive; he didn't die."

Mom looked worried. She kept asking my aunts where was everyone else. There were a total of 31 family members divided into two buses, but the other bus was nowhere in sight; and now there was only 18 of us left.

We slept at grandpa's house that night, and the next morning Dad arrived in his army uniform. I got to see Dad only once a year for about a month, and then he had to go again. I often asked Dad how come I hardly saw him at home, and he just told me that he had to go to protect us from the communists.

Mom and Dad were arguing outside. Dad yelled at mom for lying to him that grandpa died, and Mom just yelled back saying that she's saving Dad's life. Dad wanted to stay and fight, but Mom said that the country is lost and that Dad will die if he stays.

My parents saw me standing in the corner watching them fight, and Mom walked over to me and explained that we're going to America to live; and I cannot tell any strangers about it. I asked Mom where is America, and she said it's a place very far away where there are no communists and no bombs landing on us.

Then Mom turned to Dad and said Dad should make a choice . . . stay and die or go to America and live with his wife and children. Whatever choice Dad makes, Mom and the rest of us are going to America as she had planned.

Dad chose to be with his family. He took off his uniform and buried it in the yard. As he turned to me, tears were pouring from his eyes. Deep down, Dad knew that Mom was right. He had lost his country, and he didn't want to risk losing his family, too. Mom assured Dad that he had made the right decision and if the family stayed that she and Dad would certainly die, leaving children homeless and without parents.

Running Out of Time

Mom worked for the U.S. Embassy under the direction of the C.I.A. Dad worked for the South Vietnamese military intelligence. Dad's job was to intercept the enemy's messages and also to seek out those who took bribes and committed treason against the country.

On the third day, my aunt 4 from America arrived at my grandpa's house. Aunt 4 asked Mom where was the rest of the family, and Mom said she didn't know and that there's only 18 of us left. Aunt 4 said we could not wait for them any longer because time was running out, and we must leave for the U.S. Embassy right away.

Mom has six children, and she gathered all of us together to leave; but one of my younger sisters, two years younger than me, yelled and screamed that she was being kidnapped. My sister lived with grandma since she was born, and she thought that grandma was her real mother. She didn't recognize us.

Mom tried to explain to her, but she didn't believe Mom. Grandma came out and told Mom to leave my sister with her because, if we take my sister along, all her screaming and yelling would raise suspicion; and we might be captured by the communists. And besides, if we died, at least my sister will be alive. Dad agreed and Mom resented him for agreeing, but she knew that my sister would endanger us.

At the Embassy

As we arrived at the U.S. Embassy, aunt 4's husband was waiting for us at the gate. That's the first time I had ever seen him. He was this big white man in an American soldier's uniform. We took the stairway to the top of the U.S. embassy. Halfway up, I was tired; and my aunt's husband picked me up and carried me all the way to the roof top. On the roof top, there were lines of people waiting to get into the long helicopters, which my family referred to as the flying caterpillars.

When it was our turn, there were two helicopters in front of us. An American soldier split our family into two groups of nine and pointed to both helicopters. I saw my aunt arguing with him, and then her husband came and talked to the soldier. My aunt explained to us that the soldier split us up so that if one helicopter goes down, half of the family would still survive. She then told him that she wanted to keep everyone together, and it's either we live together or die together.

The people in line behind us said to us "if you're not going first then we're going first," and the soldier pointed them into the first helicopter and directed our family, all 18 of us, into the second helicopter.

As I climbed into the helicopter, another American soldier smiled at me. He was sitting by the door with a big long gun, and I have never seen so many bullets in my life hanging out on the side of the gun. I sat near him and kept on marveling at this big gun he had. I was curious.

After a few moments, both helicopters took off at almost the same time. We looked down at the city, and everything was burning. All of a sudden, the helicopter in front of us exploded and went down in flames; then my aunts all started to scream and cry and shout that we're all going to die.

Then the soldier next to me started screaming and yelling in a language that I didn't understand as he pulled the trigger on the big gun he was holding. He sounded angry; and the more he shot at the people below, the more he screamed in the strange language. I leaned over to look out to see what he was shooting at, and he shoved me back and screamed at me and pointed to the nets hanging along the wall of the helicopter. Grabbing my arm, he forced me to hang on to it.

I sat there and watched everyone cry and looked at the bullet shells landing on the floor of the helicopter. After a few moments of the helicopter twisting and turning, the soldier stopped shooting and everything was quiet.

To America

We landed in Thailand, at least my aunts told us it was Thailand; and we stayed there for two days. Then a gigantic boat came, and everyone was taken on board. It was the *U.S.S. Hancock.*

Everyone filled up the boat fast, and I stood and watched as soldiers pushed the helicopters over the edge of the boat into the ocean to make room for more people. We were all packed like sardines in cans, and it was very hot inside the boat. Then the nice soldiers came by and took fans and fanned the place by hand and opened the round windows to cool us down.

I was holding a Vietnamese Dong (Vietnamese money) in my hand, and a nice soldier came by with an apple and traded me the apple for it. He also gave me some milk to drink.

We reached Guam and stayed there for several days; and from there, we flew on a big airplane to America. I felt sick and threw up all over the plane because it was moving so fast.

When we reached America, the lights were so beautiful. There were lights everywhere, and I'd never seen so many cars in my life. The people I saw in America all spoke the language I didn't understand. Even my aunt 4 spoke the same language. Mom cried a happy cry and said we were safe and free at last.

Years later, I asked Mom what would have happened if our family didn't make it to America. Mom just looked at us and said that if we didn't make it, we would probably be dead. Before we left, Mom had bought poison and her intent was, if we never made it to the U.S. Embassy, to return to our house and have our last meal together because she would rather die with her family than us being separated and tortured and killed by the communists.

Well, I'm glad we survived, and I'm thankful everyday for everyone who risked their lives to let us have a taste of freedom that can only be found in America.

A Hazardous Boat Escape

Tran Thi My Ngoc

In the following selection Tran Thi My Ngoc describes her escape from Vietnam. Fearing the torture, imprisonment, and hard labor of the Communist reeducation camps, thousands of Vietnamese fled their country from 1978 to 1981. Those who were able to escape did so on leaky, ramshackle boats, and often paid monumental ransoms for their passage. Many families pooled resources to send relatives ahead, hoping their success would secure passage for the others. Refugees like Tran Thi My Ngoc faced many dangers during the journey. If they made it past Vietnamese Communist officials, they faced starvation, exposure, disease, piracy, and drowning. Even worse, nearby countries such as Thailand, Indonesia, and Malaysia did not guarantee asylum, and many boats were denied safe harbor. The plight of these refugees, often referred to as "boat people," garnered world media attention. In at least one case, such attention helped procure international aid.

Tran Thi My Ngoc describes how the people on her boat were robbed and abused by pirates, how seasick she became, and how she was finally rescued by the Malaysian navy. Tran Thi My Ngoc is an author, translator, and social worker.

On the twenty-fifth of December in 1979, I was supposed to leave Saigon to go to Can Tho. So on the twenty-fourth my Mom bought Christmas food, like we usually would have. Vietnamese celebrate everything. More so because we are more Westernized than other people. So at Christmas we would have a tree and go partying and come back and eat at midnight. We didn't go partying after 1975, though, because of the Communists. So my mom made Christmas dinner early because I would be leaving on the twenty-fifth. We had sweet bread, ham, and chicken and everything. All the goodies we usually ate.

I was so cross with my mom. It hurt me deeply that I had to leave and I didn't know how to express it. The big Christmas dinner just made it all that harder for me. And I couldn't say it. I knew she did it for me, but I couldn't eat a thing, nor could anybody. Everybody knew that once I was gone there would be no return, and it might be the last time that I saw them or they saw me. The Christmas dinner that year was more like a funeral than a celebration.

To prepare me for the trip my mom gave me an American one-hundred-dollar bill and some jewels. We knew that in the refugee camps jewels were good. Every kid in the family always has jewels, so I took three rings; one of them was twenty-four karat gold. The one hundred dollars was for when I got to America.

My mom sewed the money and the rings into the seams of my clothes. Then I had to disguise myself. Can Tho is the countryside, not a cosmopolitan town. People there are different from people in Saigon. I was to dress as a laborer, wearing black pajamas and a conical hat.

On the next morning I was trying not to cry, but you show grief even if not tears. My mom was crying. She hid behind a door. My mom hugged me and my sisters hugged me and they had to act normal because the Fifth Column people [Communist sympathizers] were watching. Then I just walked out the door and never looked back. I got on the bus going south to Can Tho. I was supposed to wait in the bus station in Can Tho for someone to come for me. But night came and nobody came for me. I had to sleep on the floor of the bus station on a piece of newspaper. The night was so long.

Boarding the Boat

Finally, along with other people who came to Can Tho to get on the boat, someone took us to a house that belonged to the man who had the boat. They fed us and we waited for dark again. That night we went to the port where there were these little boats. We got onto the little boats—the first time in my life I had been on one. I was so scared I would fall off. There were ten of us in each of these small boats. They carried us out to another boat. So we got from the little boat onto a bigger boat, which had then maybe twenty some people in there. We were packed in like sardines. We waited that night. I don't know if you have ever been on the river at night. It was my first time. The moon was shining. We were keeping so quiet. A baby on the boat cried and her voice carried up and down the river and all over the place. People were terrified because they thought the baby would attract the Communists who patrolled the rivers at night looking for people like us, people trying to escape.

So we whispered, "Please do something about the baby. Give it something." The baby was lucky it didn't get killed at that moment. Finally they gave him something to drink to sleep; cough syrup.

The boat took us to another boat and in that boat there were about fifty of us, still like sardines. They piled up co-conuts and watermelons on the other side to look like they were merchants, and we were all crowded in the middle. We didn't have water to drink. We waited all day on that boat. In the morning it was so hot. We couldn't go to the toilet and there was nothing to eat.

Finally on the night of the twenty-ninth the boat was ready, so we were taken further down the river. I tell you it was awful sitting in that boat. It was so hot and crowded and we were all hungry and uncomfortable.

We got into another, bigger boat. It was worse. The river breaks into tributaries. That night we were really quiet because we were ready to go, and a patrol boat came over and said, "Who's in there?" And the two guys acted like fishermen and said, "Nobody, just us fishermen waiting for morning." They said, "Are you sure, just the two of you?" And they used the lamp to look. They finally went away. The boat started to move to the bigger tributary that was closer to the river mouth at the sea.

My heart was beating so fast. Finally we got close to the mouth of the river, to another big boat. We went to that boat and got on board.

Now the crew on this boat didn't know anything about navigating their stupid boat. There was only one guy who had gone out on the sea before—he was a Navy man and was the only one who knew how to read a compass; the only one who knew anything, really. The rest of the crew did not know anything. We did not know about this until we were in deep trouble. If my mother knew about this before, she wouldn't have let me go.

The engine was running so loud, and the night was so still. Too much noise would attract the patrol. Finally the boat got out safely to the sea.

A Run-In with Officials

I stayed in the bottom of the boat. There were people on the top. I was so seasick. They looked back and suddenly there was the patrol boat coming after us. We said, "Oh, my God, those special police are coming for us. We have to stop or they'll fire." So we stopped. They came over and said, "Okay, you guys are going to escape, right?" There was no way to say no. We said "Yes." And then the guy said, "Well, what do you guys have?" I said, "Would you like some money?" They said, "Lucky for you there were only two of us on this boat." We collected gold and gave them the gold. Also there was a radio on board and they took that, too. Then they left us alone. I guess that was my farewell to Vietnam, bribing Communist officials one last time.

Now we were at sea and the stupid crew didn't know where we were going. They didn't know what international waters were, or where Malaysia was. There were high seas. I was so seasick.

Then we saw a big ship and the stupid crew members said, "Now we are in the international waters; now we are safe. Here is a ship. We will ask them to help." They threw up two flares. At that time I was moving up to the upper part of the boat because I was so sick. They threw up the flare attracting that ship and they came closer and closer, and it was a Vietnamese boat coming back to Vietnam! I couldn't believe it.

Everybody was so scared. We saw that this was a large ship with guards from one end to another with guns. We were so mad at the crew because they threw up the flares.

They were a government fishing ship on an expedition and they just happened to come back and see us because we threw up the flares. They said through the loudspeaker to stop our engines and stay there. They got closer and said, "Okay, you guys are escaping, right?" And we said "Yes." What else could we say? I said, "Please let us go, we are only fifty people. And we have children here, too." So they said, "Well, we'll let you go if you give us all the gold and money you have." And we said, "But we were just robbed by somebody else!"

Well, some stupid guy on our boat was bringing Vietnamese money with him. I don't know why. But we gave them everything he had. . . .

Finally they were satisfied. They told us, "You got only one boat, us. So you were very lucky. Had you gone the other way further south there are like sixteen ships coming back, and you wouldn't have enough money to pay them off and they would have to take you back. We were only one ship, so we will let you go." And the stupid crew people—you won't believe this—asked them, "Can you tell us how we get from here to Malaysia?"

They said, "You guys don't know how to get to Malaysia?" And we said, "No." And they showed us how to set up our compass and gave us fish to eat, two big fish.

When they sailed away they yelled goodbye, and said, "Don't feel bad because you got robbed twice. You were lucky it was only twice!"

At that moment I was thinking one thought: How did I get into this? It was not enough that I was scared. After all, I had *paid* for this. And here the crew didn't know anything. Now we knew they didn't know how the hell to get to the place we wanted to go.

Well, anyway, the other boat showed us how to set our compass and so we did that. . . .

We went the way they told us. By the time I got out to the high seas I wasn't sick any more. I got used to it. And besides, I didn't eat anything. So I had with me a small bag where I had an extra pair of jeans and a T-shirt and some underwear. I had lost the conical hat and even my shoes. I was barefoot. I didn't care. I just wanted to get out of Vietnam. . . .

International Waters

Finally we were in the international waters. That meant we wouldn't be afraid of Vietnamese boats or ships any more. We were on our way, going to who knows where, and on the night of January 1 [1980] we sailed into Malaysian waters.

There were sharks swimming all around us, and I kept thinking, "This is it; with this crew, I am going to die for sure." I was feeling so bad for my mother for spending all her money on me. If I died, I wouldn't mind, because I had chosen to leave, but if I died at sea, my mother would not know. That thought was running in my mind constantly.

We didn't see land for I don't know how long. We ran out of water and food. I was eating lime juice all the time. I couldn't tolerate any food any more.

Many ships passed us but they didn't come near to rescue us, even though we tried to flag them down. Then one evening, around six o'clock, we flagged down a ship and it came over to us—and guess what we got this time? Thai pirates! Would you believe it? Our stupid crew did it again!

I wasn't seasick anymore and I was up on the deck breathing fresh air. I watched this ship come over to us, a big metal boat about five times bigger than our rickety boat. When they came over they were wearing knives and guns and I thought, I know a pirate when I see one and believe me, these guys were pirates.

They ordered that we put our boat closer to their boat and they threw a rope over to our boat to stabilize it. Then they made us jump from our boat to their boat. The sea was stormy that night. The waves were so big. The two boats, were smashing together and apart. Three of them jumped into our boat and made us jump into theirs. One of them was a young guy, about seventeen, who was smiling at me. He held me back. I was worried.

Actually, we really didn't know that they were going to rob us. They didn't act like they were going to. We were thinking that they would rescue us. So we were jumping. For some reason, I was praying all the time, so I didn't know why this guy was smiling at me and trying to hold me back. I was so worried. I was nineteen then, remember. And I was innocent.

Well, people were jumping onto the other boat so I just jumped with them. I hit something sharp and my toe was bleeding. I didn't feel pain, the cut was so deep. The little bag I had with one extra pair of pants of jeans and shirt, I threw over to their boat first. One girl jumped and missed and fell into the water and the boats were coming together. If she didn't get up in time she would be smashed, so we pulled her up. I don't know how I jumped that far even to this day. You couldn't calculate it. It was hit or miss. I saw that girl fall into the ocean and said, "Oh, my God." It was getting dark now and there was only the light from the big ship. We pulled her up and she was wet like a little mouse.

But we weren't all so lucky. One of the men jumped and the boats separated and he fell into the water. The boats came back so quick we couldn't get him out, and he was crushed and he died. We were feeling so bad. They made us line up and sit down in the front of the boat. Then they started robbing us. They went around and fumbled around in our clothes, trying to get money and gold.

Terror on the High Seas

Three of them stayed on our boat. There was a little girl still there who was so sick she was staying in the bottom of the boat, so they raped her—all three of them. The boat was being pushed and pulled back and forth by the waves and we could hear the water and the boats creaking, and we could hear her crying for help, just crying, and we couldn't do anything. So we just cried for her and for ourselves.

There were girls on their boat, too, and they could rape us at any time. It was so awful. It was the first time in my life I was exposed to any such violent behavior or events. I sat next to some young men and some of them talked of fighting back. I said, "This is not good: We do not have guns or anything. We could all get killed if you try to overcome them. There are three of them in our boat and five of them with us, and we don't know how many more they have below. So don't fight back.". . .

I said to myself, "This is it. I don't know what's going to happen. But if they touch me, I'm going to kill myself." I was scared, but I was calm then. If they tried to rape me

I would kill myself by jumping into the sea and drowning, I decided.

Suddenly I looked down and saw my right foot was bleeding. I didn't feel pain. Usually I feel pain. But I was so scared and trying so much to survive that I didn't feel any physical pain. I looked down and saw my big toe was bleeding so much, and I couldn't do anything. There was a little purse I always kept with me, I didn't put in the bag. My mom put in some antibiotic pills because we didn't know how life was in the camp and I might need them. I kept that purse and I think those pills kept me alive.

After they finished robbing us and raping the little girl, they pushed us back to our boat. They made us jump back. They made holes in the boat, broke everything, took the compass, took the map, the flashlight, and everything. We were happy because they made us jump back, because that meant they were not going to kill us.

When we got into the boat water was coming into the boat and we were sinking. It was night. It was raining. It was storming. And they left us there to die.

Saving a Sinking Ship

We had big bamboo shoots, and we were searching for the guy who fell down in the sea earlier. It couldn't have been more than an hour, but it seemed like an eternity to me. We called his name and dropped those things in in case he was there. I think deep down we knew he had died, but we called his name and dropped things that floated so in case he came back up he could hold on.

The boat was sinking, so we had to divide the people up to distribute the weight evenly and stabilize the boat. Funny how scared we were, yet we had the sense to do that—the survival instinct of human beings is incredible. The boat was tipping over and water was coming in, and this guy said, "stabilize," and we ran to the sides, divided evenly so the boat stabilized. The men started to take the water out. Lucky for us they didn't take the patching material, so the crew for once did something good and found that stuff.

After they started getting the water out, there were no lights. Somebody happened to have a match, and we'd light up and find out where the holes were that they had made. We worked real fast in concerted effort. It was unbelievable. To this day I can't believe how we did it that night.

We were still alive but we didn't see land. We didn't even know whether we were in Malaysian or Thai waters. We said by morning if we did not see land we would be dying because there was no water or food. The boat's condition was terrible. It wouldn't hold for too long. It would come apart in the water and we would all die. It was really raining and we were in the middle of the sea somewhere with no navigator. The only Navy man who knew how to use the compass and where to go had died—he was the one who fell into the sea and drowned—and the crew said, "We don't know where to go. How do we go?" And we said, "You mean you guys don't know where to go?" My God, I thought I was dying ten times over.

Finally, everybody was so tired they said forget it, and the boat just drifted and we all waited to die. The engine didn't work because water got into the engine. Lucky for us there was no big typhoon, just heavy rain.

We just let the boat drift and tried to go the way the Navy guy told us to go. He had set the compass, but now they just guessed. So we drifted through the whole night, the longest night in my life. I didn't sleep.

Have you ever felt that the night has been so long and you are so scared and so alone and you want to see the light, just any light? The darkness itself is so overwhelming. That night I couldn't wait to see a ray of light. I said, "Just let me die in the sunlight."

And morning finally came.

"No More Refugees"

It was such a warm and comforting feeling to see the sun come up. Finally we saw a grey thing in the distance—land. Just a mountainous area, but we had been almost five days on the sea. An island? Who cares?

The crew finally got the engine to work. It was working like it was half dead, but it was working.

There were two Malaysian Navy ships and they were looking at us. We were feeling good now we were going to get rescued. High time, because we had run out of food and water. People were smiling. I said, "Get down. You have to act real sick and real terrible for them to help you. You can't be so happy. Who would help you then?"

The Malaysian Navy men saw us. They told us to stay away from their ships and they would get somebody to come over. They said, Don't get closer. One guy came out and examined us. I was the only one in the boat who could speak up for anything. I knew English, and next to me there was a guy who knew a little bit of English, so I was telling him what happened to our boat, that we were robbed and everything and now we're out of water and we have children and don't have food and so on, and the engine would not work.

We asked that they help us. So he went back to tell the commander of the ship. And he came back and said we could put our boat close to theirs. I was invited up to the big ship and the other guy who knew some English went with me. I went in to see the captain, and explained exactly what happened. He had been in Saigon once. He was asking me about places like the Caravelle Hotel, those big places, and I was telling them that yes, I was from Saigon and I knew them. They were checking me out.

While I was up there they started feeding the people on the boat, giving them water and food to eat. I was barefooted and I had not had a shower since the twenty-seventh, and I had not had the time to comb my hair. I was a total mess. I was vain, being a girl, so after I talked to the captain, I requested that I be able to go to a restroom. I looked at myself in the mirror and I looked like a bum. I said, "Oh, my God, is this me," I had been transformed into a street urchin.

The captain wanted us to go to Singapore because Malaysia had said, No more refugees. But our engine had stopped working again and that meant they would have to pull us out to the open sea again and set us adrift, and we might die. But they could not take us to a refugee camp. He was trying to explain to me that it was hard because he had to follow orders. I kept pleading with him.

I remember distinctly one thing I said to him. "This is a small boat. We have only fifty people. One has died and we have children. Our engine was broken. We cannot go to Singapore. We would if we could. But we can't. So please help us."

He said he would have to think about it. . . .

It was the afternoon now, so they let us rest for a while. In the evening, they said, "You have to come with us." So they attached a cable to our boat and pulled us out to the open sea because they couldn't take us. The captain was doing this and I couldn't believe it.

They pulled us out near to an island that was uninhabited. They anchored there because it was night and the sea was getting rough again. . . .

In the morning the captain came out and said he talked to headquarters and it was okay to take us to the refugee camp.

I was so happy. That was a very good thing that he did. There was no way for me to repay him. I can't even remember his face clearly today, and I am sorry about that. He said since we were only forty-nine people they would send us to a refugee camp.

So now men and women got on the ship and they pulled the boat to Pulau Bidong camp.

Let me tell you, after being at sea for so long I was really happy. It was about noon when we came to the island where the camp was.

The shore was full of people. It was so crowded I couldn't believe my eyes. I didn't know if this was a good thing happening or what. I never knew what a refugee camp was before. But we were safe after all.

I was the only one talking (talking too much), on the ship, and they said to me, You will be able to leave the camp fast because you speak English. I remember that. At that moment I really didn't care what speaking English mattered. Why would that help me?

Before they let us go, we sang for them. We stood on their deck and sang a Vietnamese song for them, all of us. It was all we could do. It was all we had left to give them— a song. It was a well-known Vietnamese song, so all of us knew it. It was about free Vietnam. A proud song.

Then they said goodbye to us, and we said goodbye and thank you to them.

We were discharged onto smaller boats, because the ship couldn't go closer to the island because of the coral. At that time I only had a pair of black pants and a shirt. I didn't have anything else. The other bag was lost with the pirates.

The refugees who were there before, every time there was a boat coming in they would go down to see if any of their relatives were there. So I was treading water to go in, and the coral was sharp. We didn't even have shoes on. Our boat was towed close to shore and onto shore to be broken, because they didn't want us to have a boat to go around somewhere in Malaysian waters. They wanted us to be confined there.

I waded ashore. It was just a sea of people. It was pathetic. I was standing at the shore on the beach, not knowing anything and trying to find out what was going on.

Among the people was my brother who had left before me. He came down to see if there was anybody he knew. There he was, wearing only a pair of shorts. And I was so beat up. I looked so bad.

There were 46,000 people on the island—all refugees. There was little food and little water. Life was very hard and I was working all the time. I didn't have any other clothes to wear. People lived like animals. There was no hygiene, no sanitary facilities. People had to dig holes for an outhouse. It was awful, awful, awful.

The Malaysians tried to prevent boats from landing there. They would tow them out to sea. The boats would sink and the people would drown. In the morning, we would go down to the beach and there would be bodies everywhere—men, women, and children. All Vietnamese. We would bury them every morning. They were the unlucky ones.

I was so deficient in vitamins that I got bloated. My face was all blown up and watery.

I was on Pulau Bidong for three and a half months. And it's there I learned how people behave when they are desperate. People could kill for a little food or for a little money. Friends turned into enemies in a matter of seconds. I cried so often. I couldn't sleep. I just slept two or three hours a night. I just stared at the sky. I was feeling so bad for myself, for everything, for people.

All of my energy was put into living, surviving, and getting out. I didn't care where I would go, I just wanted to get out of the camp. I had to stay alive.

CBS News came to the island and filmed a program there. I think Ed Bradley was there filming. And you know what happened after that? I think the Malaysian government was criticized about what was going on. Because of that CBS program we started getting better rations. CBS let the world know what the refugee camp was like and what was happening to the boat people. After that we got enough to eat. It came in a package: rice and tea and food. From the United Nations. God bless the United Nations! Each person got a small bag of food every three days. It actually came faster than we could eat it because we were so used to starving for so long.

My brother and I found sponsors and were cleared to go to the United States. We were supposed to leave on the nineteenth of April.

Sponsorship in the United States

At last I was leaving. I didn't even know then where I was going. I knew I was going to the United States of America, but I didn't know where in the United States.

When I was in the transit camp, they told me I was going to Iowa. I didn't know where Iowa was. They took out a map and pointed to a place and said, "Here's Iowa, in the Midwest." I didn't really understand, but I said, "Okay, Iowa. Fine."

I was sponsored by a church. I landed in Des Moines with about three hundred other Vietnamese. The governor of the state was there to welcome us. Then they matched each of us up to the place we were supposed to go, and they drove us to our new homes. They drove us across Iowa. I remember going through this town on a Sunday evening and there was not a soul in the streets. It was beautiful. It was cold and gray, too. I wondered where we were going and why there were no people in Iowa.

They put me in an apartment that night. I couldn't sleep. I had nightmares. Every time there was a noise outside I would panic. All noises scared me. I remembered the noise of the motor of the Thai pirates on the sea—and I would wake up immediately and be paralyzed with fear and be sweating. That happened to me every night for about three months.

Well, I am coming to my happy ending. The young girl who was raped by the Thai pirates is now living in Canada. She is married now and happy. She was such a sweet little girl. I was so glad things turned out all right.

My brother graduated from the university in Iowa and is now an engineer. I graduated from the university there and earned my master's degree in social work in California. Then I returned to Pulau Bidong and worked with the new refugees and boat people after I earned my degree.

Looking back today, it seems unreal. That's why I had to go back to work in a refugee camp. It was a way not only to help other people, but to let them know that there is a future in the free world for them.

But also I had to go back to heal myself. In that period of time I was living but I was really like a dead person. I just functioned with no emotions. After I survived, I still needed healing. Helping others who went through what I went through and worse has provided that healing.

So today I am not only a survivor. I am also alive.

CHAPTER 2

The First Waves of Immigrants Adapt to Their New Home

COMING TO AMERICA

Life in U.S. Refugee Camps

Gail Paradise Kelly

The route to the United States for most Vietnamese refugees was less than direct. Many moved through refugee camps in Guam, Thailand, or the Philippines before landing in one of the four transitional camps opened on the U.S. mainland in 1975 after the North Vietnamese took over South Vietnam. Families shared barracks, and in some cases tents, with little privacy. However, the camps worked to unify families split apart by the war and provided services that helped the residents adjust to American culture. In these camps the Vietnamese began the transformation from being refugees to being immigrants.

In this selection author Gail Paradise Kelly describes the organization and operation of the American camps. The camps provided child care, English lessons, college placement, and also worked to settle the immigrants in various regions throughout the United States. Kelly, former chair of the Department of Educational Organization, Administration, and Policy in the Graduate School of Education at the University of Buffalo, was also a pioneer in the field of feminist education. She died in 1991.

Vietnamese did not travel directly from their country to the place they ultimately settled in the United States. Most, when they left Vietnam, either landed in or were brought to American overseas bases like Utapo in Thailand (where Vietnamese air force pilots flew their planes) and Subic

Gail Paradise Kelly, *From Vietnam to America: A Chronicle of the Vietnamese Immigration to the United States.* Boulder, CO: Westview Press, 1977. Copyright © 1977 by Westview Press. All rights reserved. Reproduced by permission of the Literary Estate of Gail Paradise Kelly.

Bay and Clark Field in the Philippines. From these bases most were flown to Wake [Island] or Guam, where Americans, as of 22 April [1975], had set up a reception center to house 50,000 refugees for a maximum of 90 days. By 26 April the facility at Guam had become severely overcrowded. Further, because of the unanticipated numbers of refugees who arrived at U.S. bases, it was apparent that processing and resettling of immigrants could not be done from Guam within three months. The center at Guam was considered unsafe over the long run because of typhoons that could hit the island. Thus, four centers, or camps, were established on the U.S. mainland to house Vietnamese while they waited for clearance to enter the United States or some third country. Camp Pendleton, outside of San Diego, California, opened on 29 April with a tent city capable of housing 18,000 immigrants. On 2 May Fort Chaffee opened in Arkansas, with barracks that could accommodate 24,000 persons. Eglin Air Force Base, with a capacity for housing 5,000 persons, was the third reception center, opening on 4 May 1975. On 28 May, the fourth and last reception center, Fort Indian Town Gap, near Harrisburg, Pennsylvania, opened with the capacity to house more than 16,000 refugees.

In the camps, Vietnamese were "processed" into America: they were interviewed, examined, given identification numbers, registered with American agencies, introduced to American society and culture, and found a place to live and work in the U.S. Vietnamese went into the camps as refugees; they came out of the camps as immigrants. As refugees they were a chapter in Vietnamese history and culture; when they emerged from the camps, they had begun a series of painful adjustments that severed them from Vietnamese life as they knew it and were on the road to becoming Vietnamese-Americans. The camps were the places where systematic efforts began at resocializing Vietnamese to live in America and accommodate to the country and its culture. . . .

An Introduction to American Life

The camps paved the way for Vietnamese entry to the United States; they also introduced them to American life, often in well-organized programs. The nightly movies and daily newspapers put out by camp management as well as public school for children ages six to eighteen, adult classes in the English language and vocational skills, and "orientation" meetings all tried to prepare Vietnamese for the United States, informing them how to date, prepare food, speak to Americans, work, and play.

The camps prepared people to live and work in American society; they also settled Vietnamese throughout the country. Camp management . . . pursued a policy of diaspora. Resettlement was aimed at preventing large clusters of Vietnamese, Cambodians, or Laotians from building up in any given area in the country. After the immigrants were found sponsors, the camps closed. . . .

American Service Organizations

American service groups, at the invitation of the senior civilian coordinator, ran extensive programs which complemented the work of resettlement agencies and helped in the day-to-day operation of the camps. Organizations like the Red Cross and the YMCA offered many services to immigrants. The Red Cross, for example, held baby-care classes for mothers and expectant parents; it ran a college placement and an educational credentials translation service; it also, with the YMCA, staffed recreation halls in the camps that ran ping-pong tournaments, organized teenage dances and art shows, provided sewing machines for individuals to use, and furnished reading rooms with English language tutors. One of the Red Cross' most extensive services was family reunification. At Fort Indian Town Gap, two individuals working full time for the Red Cross interviewed individuals who had lost family members in the evacuation of Vietnam, took down the names of these lost relatives and checked them against lists of Vietnamese in camps in Thailand, Hong Kong, and within the U.S. If it located individuals, the Red Cross would notify the State Department, which decided whether the family should be unified. The State Department would provide for reunification only if it involved bringing together members of nuclear families. No more than seven members of a family would be reunified. Over 300 Vietnamese families at Fort Indian Town Gap were reunited through Red Cross efforts. . . .

The U.S. Army psychological operations unit at Fort Indian Town Gap produced the camp's daily newspaper *Dat Lanh* which not only informed Vietnamese of the rules and regulations of the camp, but also ran article after article on life in the United States. It was the army at Fort Indian Town Gap which decided who would have access to the camp from the outside and handled much of the public relations for the camp. The army also made the rules about the hours during which civilians, including those employed at the camp, could be present in areas of the camp in which immigrants could move freely, and kept school personnel, resettlement agency case workers, etc., apart from the immigrants they theoretically served.

The civilian coordinator, in addition to coordinating the work of the various government and private agencies, had an organization all his own which, in conjunction with the military, governed Vietnamese in the camp. Except for Eglin Air Force Base in Florida, which held a relatively small number of immigrants (about 5,000 at its height) and was open for but a short time (less than two months), the camps were small cities housing more than 26,000 persons over several square miles. Each camp was divided into "areas" or districts for the sake of day-to-day governance; each area was superintended by an area coordinator appointed by the senior civilian coordinator and a military officer who handled security and logistics. Each area coordinator's office had a staff of secretaries and interpreters who were assisted in their functions by immigrants. . . .

Vietnamese Assistants

The Vietnamese assistants, or barracks chiefs, had little authority of their own. Their role was to organize individuals to maintain their barracks (clean toilets, take out garbage, sweep stairs, etc.) and inform Vietnamese of clothing supply and meal ticket distribution and any other information that area coordinators needed to have distributed to each individual living in the camp. The barracks chief also was theoretically the immigrants' representative to each area coordinator. He was supposed to bring problems to the attention of area coordinators who would then attempt to solve them. These problems ranged from interfamily conflicts over noise, lights, or property within a barracks or tent to intra-family difficulties and fights such as wife beating. Sometimes the barracks chiefs identified troublemakers (thieves, dissidents, noncooperators, etc.) for area coordinators.

The area coordinator's role was to tend to the daily physical needs of immigrants. One area coordinator described this work as that of "handing out toothpaste." But in fact the job was never that mundane, partly because of area coordinators' backgrounds and their conceptions of their work. The area coordinators at Fort Indian Town Gap were all former AID [Agency for International Development] employees who had worked together for several years in Vietnam out of the consul general's office in Da-Nang. At least two were fluent in Vietnamese. All had served as district or provincial advisors either in land reform programs or political organizing projects. One had been in Vietnam since 1967; another since 1968; and a third since 1972. Area coordinators at other camps had similar backgrounds.

The area coordinator's official role was to maintain order within the day-to-day life of immigrants and to provide immigrants with housing, clothing, and food. Their role also was to support the overall camp effort of resettling Vietnamese in America. The area coordinators encouraged Vietnamese to attend camp activities believed to speed resettlement, particularly English language classes and cultural orientation sessions. Through the barracks chiefs, the area coordinators announced the classes and events and eventually singled out refugees who needed to be encouraged to attend such functions. The area coordinators also assisted in decisions on the pace of resettlement. They pressured Vietnamese into accepting sponsorship offers by explaining to them the reality facing them. This often amounted to pointing out that the camps were going to close down soon and that the immigrants would not be able to continue living in them. . . .

[The camps] were also places where many Vietnamese received their first exposure to American society and the demands they would have to meet to survive in it. The mode of camp management made it clear to Vietnamese that Americans, not Vietnamese, held power within the country and that Vietnamese would have to conform to American ways of doing things. While this is apparent in camp organization and routine, it is clearest in the cultural programs in the camps which, more than anything else, tried to define for Vietnamese their future patterns of life, thought, and culture. These patterns suggested very little possibility of Vietnamese maintaining their own communities. Rather, they emphasized Vietnamese becoming Americans. In this sense, Vietnamese were being asked to transform themselves from refugee to immigrant. Refugees were persons who remained closely allied to the culture from which they came and were away from home for political reasons. A refugee is a temporary resident abroad. An immigrant, however, is a permanent resident of a new country not his or her own who, because of this permanency, develops new cultural roots—not necessarily those of his new country's mainstream, but not those of his home country either. The camps' organization, routines, and educational programs promoted the transformation from refugee to immigrant.

The Dispersion Policies

Hien Duc Do

According to Hien Duc Do in the following selection, the American public's response to the influx of Vietnamese into the United States after the fall of Saigon in 1975 was a mixture of empathy, guilt (due to American involvement in the Vietnam War), and at times hostility. Fear that a concentration of refugees in any one region would be an economic drain on the receiving communities led to the formation of refugee dispersion policies. After the Vietnamese were resettled throughout the United States, many first-wave refugees undertook a second migration, during which they relocated to other parts of the country. California became a popular destination because of its warm weather, which was similar to Vietnam's, and its plenitude of jobs. Hien Duc Do is an associate professor and chair of the social science department at San Jose State University in San Jose, California.

The Vietnamese exodus and their resettlement in the United States could not have come at a worse time in U.S. history. The Vietnam War was an extremely unpopular war at home: 57,692 American men and women had died and 2,500 were listed as missing in action or as prisoners of war. The war divided the nation deeply.

Indeed, the general attitude of the American public at the end of the war was one of hostility toward the Vietnamese refugees. A Gallup Poll taken in May 1975 showed "54 percent of all Americans opposed to admitting Vietnamese refugees to live in the United States and only 36

Hien Duc Do, *The Vietnamese Americans*. Westport, CT: Greenwood Press, 1999. Copyright © 1999 by Hien Duc Do. All rights reserved. Reproduced by permission of the publisher.

percent were in favor with 12 percent undecided". A common concern of the American public was one of economic self-interest—fear of having jobs taken away as well as having too much public assistance and welfare given to the refugees. During this time, the United States was in a period of recession with an unemployment rate of 8.3 percent. In fact, on April 27, 1975, over 60,000 angry unemployed union members poured into the Robert F. Kennedy stadium in Washington, D.C., to protest the lack of employment opportunities. The May 12, 1975, issue of *Newsweek* quoted California Congressman Burt Talcott as having said, "Damn it, we have too many Orientals already. If they all gravitate to California, the tax and welfare rolls will get overburdened and we already have our share of illegal aliens." The same issue reported this statement by an Arkansas woman: "They say it is a lot colder here than in Vietnam. With a little luck, maybe all those Vietnamese will take pneumonia and die." Even liberal Democrats such as California Governor Edmund Brown and Senator George McGovern said negative things about the entire refugee operation. Several early studies documented that a substantial number of Americans preferred the exclusion of the refugees from the United States. Apart from specific conditions resulting from the Vietnam War and the economic recession, this hostile reception given by the American public represented a continuation of racism and hostility toward immigrant minority groups that has prevailed and been well documented throughout the United States' history.

Hostility Toward Asians

The Vietnamese refugees, therefore, arrived in the United States with a legacy of hostility directed toward Asians. Most of the hostility was racially and economically based. Despite these attitudes, many other Americans extended humanitarian aid and sponsored families from refugee camps. There were those who did not want them here because of the war, the economic competition, racism, and other factors. There were also others who felt responsible for their arrival and were motivated for humanitarian reasons. . . .

When Vietnamese refugees first arrived in April 1975, the U.S. government had to organize temporary refugee camps in order to transfer refugees into American society or to find third-country sponsors as soon as possible. As a result, there were four camps that were quickly set up to handle the estimated number of arrivals. All of the camps were on military bases, since the bases were able to provide the necessary labor and space to accommodate large numbers of refugees. The first camp to open was at Camp Pendleton in California, followed by camps at Fort Chaffee in Arkansas, Eglin Air Force Base in Florida, and finally, Indiantown Gap in Pennsylvania. . . .

The camps succeeded in providing the basic necessities of daily life while Vietnamese refugees were adjusting and waiting to be sponsored out of camps.

Refugee Dispersion Policy

To minimize the social impact of the large influx of Vietnamese refugees on an American public that did not favor the Vietnam War, the U.S. federal government, under the leadership of President Gerald Ford, adapted the Refugee Dispersion Policy. The administration arrived at the policy after President Ford consulted a number of people around the country. In order for the policy to be accepted, President Ford personally lobbied members of Congress, members of his own cabinet, and other prominent community leaders around the country. The Refugee Dispersion Policy served four purposes: to relocate the Vietnamese refugees as quickly as possible so that they could achieve financial independence; to ease the impact of a large group of refugees on a given community to avoid an increase in competition for jobs; to make it logistically easier to find sponsors; and to prevent the development of an ethnic ghetto. Given the political and social climate of the United States at the time, the influential factors leading to this Dispersion Policy were primarily political and financial, not social. It was felt that if this policy was carried out successfully, the Vietnamese refugees would quickly assimilate into American society.

Nine voluntary agencies (VOLAGS) were contracted by the government's Interagency Task Force to handle the resettlement of the refugees in the United States. The agencies included the United Hebrew Immigration and Assistance Service, the Lutheran Immigration and Refugee Service, the International Rescue Committee, Church World Service, the American Funds for Czechoslovak Refugees, the United States Catholic Conference, the Travelers Aid International Social Service, and the Council for Nationalities Service. While in refugee camps, each family was asked to choose a resettlement agency. If the family did not have a preference, one was assigned.

The primary task of these voluntary agencies was to find sponsors that would have the ability to fulfill both financial and moral responsibilities and to match them with each refugee's families or individuals. The responsibilities of the sponsors included providing temporary food, clothing and shelter, assistance in finding employment or job training for the head of the household, enrolling the children in school, and, finally, providing ordinary medical care. In other words, the sponsors would serve as a resource to introduce the Vietnamese refugees into the American society while they were becoming economically self-supporting.

Methods of Resettlement

There were four ways for the refugees to leave the four temporary refugee camps and enter into U.S. society: resettlement to a third country, repatriation to Vietnam, proof of financial independence, and location of a sponsor through the voluntary agencies.

Although third-country resettlement was encouraged by the United States government, this avenue was rarely chosen by the Vietnamese refugees. Very few other countries offered their assistance to resettle Vietnamese refugees unless they were certified professionals in needed technical areas, had immediate relatives in that country, or could speak that country's language. These requirements were designed to discourage an influx of refugees to these countries, for it was clearly difficult for many refugees to fulfill even one of these requirements.

Only a small number of refugees chose to return to Vietnam. Darrel Montero, an anthropologist, reported that "by October 1975, repatriation had been granted to 1,546 refugees by the new government of Vietnam". Most were military men who were forced to leave their families behind at the time of their evacuation. During the chaotic final days of the war, many people were separated from their families and the whereabouts of their family members were unknown for a while. However, once some people realized that they had left their families behind, even after a very short period of time, they chose to return to Vietnam in order to be with them. Although the desire for freedom and the fear of communism were important criteria, being with their families was a much stronger bond, and many felt compelled to return to Vietnam despite the consequences that might have been waiting for them upon their return.

The third method by which the Vietnamese refugees were allowed to leave the camps was to demonstrate financial independence. A refugee family was required by the Task Force to show proof of cash reserves totaling at least $4,000 for each member. However, due to their abrupt flight from Vietnam, very few refugees could use this option. It would have been unlikely for them to have been able to obtain such a large sum of money, given the abrupt ending [of] the war. In addition, it was unlikely that many refugees would report to the authorities their financial holdings for fear of the unknown that awaited them in this new country. They had recently lost everything and were about to start from scratch. Indeed, if they were fortunate enough to have had some money or gold, it would have been wise for them to guard it in order to have a small safety net. Consequently, the first waves of Vietnamese refugees entered U.S. society primarily through the family sponsorship method.

The sponsors found by voluntary agencies consisted of congregations, parishes or affiliates, churches, individual families, corporations, small businesses, and American companies with former Vietnamese employees. In addition, if any of the refugees had relatives already living in the United States who could fulfill the same requirements (food, clothing, shelter, school enrollment, and medical care), they could qualify as sponsors as well. However, there were only 15,000 Vietnamese living in the United States before 1975. Most of these individuals were foreign exchange students on temporary visas or wives of U.S. soldiers who had served in Vietnam. In essence, there was not an already established Vietnamese American community in the United States and, therefore, this method hardly applied to the first waves of refugees.

The Orderly Departure Program

The family sponsorship method was later used more frequently, however, by first-wave refugees who sponsored family members and relatives stranded in Vietnam after 1975. This method was used through the implementation of two federal government-sponsored programs resulting from the Conference on Indochinese Refugees held in Geneva,

Switzerland, on June 14, 1980: the Orderly Departure Program and the Humanitarian Operation program.

The goal of these programs was to "provide Vietnamese a 'viable alternative' to dangerous clandestine departure by boat or over land" (Congressional Hearing). However, this viable alternative was not as successful as anticipated as many Vietnamese refugees continued to leave by boat out of desperation and in fear of persecution from the communist government. Under the Orderly Departure and Humanitarian Operation programs, there are three categories under which Vietnamese Americans with U.S. citizenship can participate in these programs: category I—family reunification, category II—former U.S. government or firm or organization employees, etc., and category III—reeducation center detainees. As a result of these avenues, many Vietnamese families who arrived during the first and second period, who now have citizenship or, at least, permanent residence status, are using the first category to bring any remaining family members to the United States. Hoai, a college junior majoring in biological sciences reports:

> My family has been trying to bring my mother's older sister over for a couple of years now. It has taken a lot of time and a lot of money because we have to bribe many of the government agencies and numerous officials in Vietnam in order for them to speed up the process and give her family the required papers. We have been waiting for the papers to clear for at least nine months. They have told us a few times that they were on the next flight out of Saigon but they have been telling us that for a few months. . . . I think we will probably receive two weeks' notice before they will arrive. It is pretty hard on our family economically and emotionally for all our family, but especially my mom.

As a result of the U.S. Federal Government Dispersion Policy, Vietnamese refugees were dispersed throughout the United States shortly upon arrival. . . .

Secondary Migration of First Wave Vietnamese

After living for a period of time with their sponsors and adjusting to the new environment, many Vietnamese refugees began to relocate to different locations throughout the United States. They did not remain in the original place of their resettlement for a number of reasons. Weather played a significant role in the formation of a secondary migration (the voluntary migration of people after a few years of their initial resettlement by voluntary organizations) initiated by Vietnamese refugees. Weather conditions that exist in many parts of the United States were substantially different from those in Vietnam. In only a few states—California, Texas, and Florida—was the climate somewhat similar to that of Vietnam.

The 1980 United States Census Data on the Vietnamese Americans in the United States indicated that the most populated states were California with 34.78 percent, Texas with 11.34 percent, Louisiana with 4.43 percent, Virginia with 3.86 percent, Washington with 3.65 percent, Pennsylvania with 3.31 percent, and Florida with 2.89 percent. Fifty percent of the entire Vietnamese refugee population lived in either California, Texas, or Louisiana. Almost two thirds (64.26 percent) lived in only seven states, including the aforementioned three states, plus Virginia (3.86 percent), Washington (3.65 percent), Pennsylvania (3.31 percent), and Florida (2.89 percent).

As the harsh winter conditions hit large cities throughout the colder parts of the United States where Vietnamese refugees were initially resettled, the desire to find a location with a warmer climate and a Vietnamese community increased. Additionally, California's reputation for having a warm climate and an abundance of unskilled jobs, especially in San Jose's "Silicon Valley," Santa Ana, and San Diego, along with the existence of small Vietnamese communities in Los Angeles and San Jose, attracted people. A total of 43 percent of Vietnamese Americans who had migrated to Orange County, California, gave "climate" as their primary reason for migrating, whereas 22 percent gave "job/finances/education" as their second reason, followed by "family nearby" with 13 percent. This secondary migration pattern is repeated often as many Vietnamese American communities have been established throughout the United States.

Sponsorship Helps the Vietnamese Settle in America

Tricia Springstubb

Tricia Springstubb explains in the following selection that transitional camps were established in the United States to help Vietnamese immigrants who had fled Vietnam in 1975. The immigrants had several routes to leaving the camps, including repatriating to another country, returning to Vietnam, proving they were self-sufficient, and finding an American sponsor. By far the most common route chosen was sponsorship. According to Springstubb, individual Americans and groups could sponsor immigrants, which usually involved helping the adults find work, enrolling the children in schools, and providing whatever help was necessary to help the newcomers succeed in America. The Vietnamese immigrants who were sponsored were grateful for the assistance, Springstubb reports. Springstubb is the author of numerous works of fiction and nonfiction.

In the weeks after the fall of Saigon [in 1975], the United States opened four transitional refugee camps on American soil. The first and largest was Camp Pendleton in southern California. The other three were Fort Chafee in Arkansas, Eglin Air Force Base in Florida, and Indiantown Gap in Pennsylvania. The camps were jointly run by the military, the government's Interagency Task Force on In-

Tricia Springstubb, *The Vietnamese Americans*. San Diego: Lucent Books, 2001. Copyright © 2001 by The Gale Group. Reproduced by permission.

dochina Refugees, and a wide range of volunteer organizations, which became known by the acronym Volags (Volunteer agencies). The Volags included among others the International Refugee Service, the YMCA, the Red Cross, and many church groups, among them the United Hebrew Immigrant Assistance Service, the Lutheran Immigration Service, and the U.S. Catholic Conference.

Upon arrival in the American camps, immigrants were interviewed and screened for security purposes, a daunting task for the officials involved. Julia Vadala Taft, who headed the Interagency Task Force, describes some of the obstacles.

> We had . . . to do security clearance [a background check to make sure the refugees were not a threat to American society]—we have a requirement in this country that if you are being brought in or are allowed to come in, either as a parolee or a refugee, you have to get your security clearances. Well, come to find out that there were a lot of agencies involved in security clearances. . . . We [the Interagency Task Force] were finding that we weren't able to process people out of the camps for two or three weeks because the security clearance process was just a nightmare.

Technicalities like this were common, and life in the American camps required a good deal of patience. Much of the immigrant's day was spent waiting in lines: for meals, for medical exams, for various forms of government processing, and for testing job skills and the English language comprehension. Translators helped determine hometowns, age, and the makeup of large family groups. In addition, the immigrants were fingerprinted by the Immigration and Naturalization Service and issued Social Security cards. During this time, families and individuals lived in large barracks or tents, which afforded little privacy. Still, adults and children alike were encouraged to attend classes, where they were instructed in English and introduced to American customs, and the plentiful food and clean water were a great improvement over the poorer conditions of most of the Asian camps [that the refugees fled to right after the fall of Saigon].

Yet many immigrants, describing their experience in the transitional camp, reported feeling discontent with their idleness and were uneasy about taking assistance from the government. Although little work was expected of them, many were eager to contribute, volunteering as translators, typists, or even cooks. At Camp Pendleton, dubbed "Operation New Arrival," the food served by military chefs—hamburgers, hot dogs, and spaghetti—caused stomach ailments among the newcomers. The Americans tried to oblige the immigrants' tastes, but in at least one case, they needed help. A *Time* magazine reporter wrote, "The Army had been supplying soggily cooked rice, but finally asked for help in its kitchens. Said a mess sergeant, 'Come and show me how to cook it properly.' A score of Vietnamese women volunteered."

Adapting to their unfamiliar environment took place not only in the mess halls, but also in the immigrants' daily contact with the American lifestyle. Entertainment, for example, was plentiful. The immigrants played volleyball, soccer, and Ping Pong. Camp officials showed American movies and sponsored concerts of American music. For the children, watching television was a fascinating way to learn about their new culture. In addition, many younger refugees spent their free time with officials and with volunteers, getting to know their adopted country on a one-on-one basis.

The camps' mission was to help those who qualified make the transition from temporary refugee to immigrant. Once the Vietnamese had received their security clearance, refugees had four main routes to leaving the camps: repatriating to another country, returning to Vietnam, proving they were self-sufficient, and finding an American sponsor. Sponsorship, ultimately became the route most Vietnamese took.

Sponsorship

Sponsoring an immigrant family was a substantial undertaking. American volunteer sponsors pledged to provide food, clothing, and shelter until the family became self-supporting. In addition, sponsors agreed to help the adults find work, to enroll the children in school, and to be available in any way to assist adaptation to American daily life. Although the government gave limited financial assistance, most of the responsibility fell on the sponsor. Andrew X. Pham was ten years old when his family fled Vietnam. He describes what sponsorship meant to him and his family:

> The First Baptist church of Shreveport, Louisiana, was our bridge to America. They loaned us the airfares. They rented us one of the church properties, found Dad work, and generally took care of the family, making sure our transition to America was comfortable. . . . [At Christmas they gave us] our very first turkey . . . for our holiday feast. Mom said it was the biggest and funniest-looking chicken she had ever seen. Everything in America is big, she said, marveling.

The job of the sponsors was made more challenging by the 1975 U.S. economic recession. Many Americans were feeling a financial strain and had little extra to spare. As a result, most sponsors were not individuals but groups. Some corporations that had previously employed the immigrants in Vietnam, including Pan Am, Bank of America, and the *New York Times*, offered to hire them at American offices. Other companies, eager to employ cheap labor, also became sponsors. A consortium of Volags also took on the task of matching refugees and sponsors. These volunteer agencies were assisted by a network of church groups. Local congregations from all across the country agreed to sponsor families.

An elderly woman from rural South Vietnam who immigrated with her family in 1975 was sponsored by a church. She recalls,

> Our sponsor rented us a two-bedroom townhouse. . . . Because a church member owned it, the rent was low. . . . The church provided everything for us: pots, bowls, dishes, a small washing machine . . . all of our needs were met. . . . The minister of the church and his son also helped us move and showed me how to use appliances that were new to me, such as the washing machine and the electric stove. The market was close by, so my husband would ride there on his bicycle and bring back food. Around noon, I would go to my sponsor's house to work on the garden we had started. . . . My sponsor bought us a gas lawn mower, and this enabled my youngest son to cut grass to earn money while attending school. . . . We are strange to them, but they helped us. That's very nice; that's precious.

The Legacy of the Camps

The transitional camps had taken on an enormous task. At Camp Pendleton alone, more than 7 million meals were served, and 165 babies were born. Yet the chief focus of the camps had always been to move the Vietnamese out as quickly and as efficiently as possible. Julia Vadala Taft, director of the Interagency Task Force on Indochina Refugees, wanted all the camps to be closed by Christmas. In an interview published in a 1996 issue of *Vietnam* magazine, she remembered, "I wanted these people [the immigrants] to celebrate their very first American Christmas in their own homes. . . . That was the goal. We let the voluntary agencies know that this was something we wanted, and so we kept the pressure on them to speed up the processing." Taft's goal became reality. By December 20, 1975, all four camps had closed.

The Second Wave

Michael P. Smith and Bernadette Tarallo

The first wave of Vietnamese immigrants to the United States tended to be well-educated government officials used to city life. These immigrants, who arrived between 1975 and 1978, tended to do well in America. In contrast, the second wave of refugees, who left Vietnam after 1978, tended to be less-educated people from rural areas. Without the skills of the first-wave immigrants, these Vietnamese Americans tended to do less well. Within the Vietnamese immigrant community these two groups remained isolated from each other.

In this selection Michael P. Smith, a professor of community studies at the University of California, Irvine, and Bernadette Tarallo, a research sociologist at the University of California, Irvine, explain how difficult it was for the second-wave immigrants to find success in America.

The Resettlement of Southeast Asian refugees in Sacramento, Calif., offers a pointed example of the social practices by which new immigrants are shaping the emerging U.S. urban landscape. This reterritorialization has created problems, as well as opportunities, within the Vietnamese migrant community. The practice of similar customs and traditions by both first- and second-wave immigrants from Vietnam to Sacramento conceals real differences between their patterns of adaptation to American life. The diversity often is masked by the promotion by the popular media of the Vietnamese as the contemporary model minority through images of strong family unity, children as valedictorians, and successful businessmen, as well as in the academic literature measuring economic adjustment. In fact, discussing the Vietnamese by extrapolating from the backgrounds and experiences of the most well-equipped first-wave settlers tends to ignore the splits both within and between them and second-wave refugees, masking many adjustment difficulties, particularly among the latter.

Although often exaggerated and oversimplified, the adjustment of the first wave is attributable in part to their social backgrounds in Vietnam—many refugees were from urban areas, educated, with professional and military experience. Although their occupational skills from Vietnam were not immediately transferable, a number eventually were able to adapt their abilities and skills to jobs where there was some carry-over after developing a functional command of the English language. Their relatively high educational and occupational backgrounds, plus their familiarity with urban living and exposure to Western culture, helped to contribute to their relatively successful adaptation.

The Isolation of Second-Wave Refugees

The situation of second-wave refugees has been quite different. Arriving from 1979 onward, they generally are less educated, not as well off financially, and often from rural areas with limited exposure to Western culture or to a technical and urbanized way of life. In many cases, illiteracy and the concept of classroom learning, particularly in acquiring English language skills, is a major obstacle. Frequently, these refugees were ethnically Chinese minorities in Vietnam who had faced past discrimination there, particularly since the fall of Saigon [to the Communists after the Vietnam War]. Furthermore, the conditions of their escape left second-wave boat people with few financial resources, deep emotional scars, and in many more ways less prepared than the first wave to make a smooth transition.

Our research, based on in-depth, ethnographic interviews with second-wave immigrants in Sacramento, is revealing that they tend to be isolated, not only from the mainstream society, but from first-wave settlers in their own community. For example, we are finding surprisingly little use of or involvement by second-wave refugees in established local Vietnamese associations and the services they offer. The differences in the backgrounds between second- and first-wave settlers—stemming not only from economic, social, and ethnic factors, but from the vast regional differences found in Vietnam—often make it difficult for them to relate to each other. Moreover, given the political conditions in Vietnam, the second wave often displays a distrust of former government officials found in the first wave, who tend to dominate Vietnamese associations and clubs. Perhaps most significant, according to an active Vietnamese community member and social worker for Child Protective Services, first-wave settlers running the Sacramento Vietnamese associations tend to lose sight of, or are out of touch with, the concerns and problems facing the majority community of second-wave immigrants. Among the key areas are those confronting youth in attempting to figure out what it means to be both Vietnamese and American. Lack of knowledge about and/or inability to identify with the perceived purpose and interests of Vietnamese associations has contributed to the second wave's lack of participation in formal social networks created by the first wave, further increasing their isolation.

Part of the isolation experienced by second-wave settlers may be attributed to the nature of the Sacramento community. Although many second-wave immigrants tend to settle in the Lemon Hill neighborhood, there is no overarching Vietnamese organization or even industry—such as electronics in San Jose, Calif.—binding them together.

If participation in formal networks by second-wave immigrants has been minimal, the creation and use of informal ones also is weak. The majority of respondents have reported that they do not know their neighbors, whether Asian or Anglo, except for passing hellos.

The emerging pattern for second-wave settlers is an extreme reliance on the immediate family in its various stages of construction, as many families only now [in 1993] are being unified through the Orderly Departure Program, and on government services to which they are entitled. These are sorely inadequate, as incoming refugee aid is limited to four months, in comparison to the 18 months of benefits available to most first-wave refugees. Older parents tend to supplement welfare with informal work in jobs where English-speaking ability is not essential, such as gardening, restaurant work, sewing, and cosmetology. Parents place their hopes for success on their children. After initially receiving welfare, the offspring tend to get jobs to put themselves through school and contribute to the family income. This heavy reliance on familial networks is placing a strain on relations within the Vietnamese family, as well as on youth in their self-formation and in making choices in the wider society.

Parenting in a New Society

Parents' concern for and lack of control over their children's behavior in the new society is overwhelming. Typical is one mother's response when asked if it is more difficult to raise children in the U.S. than in Vietnam: "Yes, I think so because it's so free in America. I feel that I don't have that much control over my children since I can't afford to pay for their education. It's not like in Vietnam; I pay for their education, so they have to listen to me. Also, my children are [self-sufficient]; I have no control over when and where they go. The time they spend at home is minimal. They can't do that in Vietnam; they have to be home after school. Furthermore, since my children were not so financially independent, they had to ask me for money to buy certain things. Therefore, I had more control and supervision over them."

Another respondent, a father, put it even more pointedly: "According to my understanding, in the American way of life, children have many misguided thoughts. They are free in an excessive sense. [Life] experience is very expensive to buy. Vietnamese say 'a child disobey their parents, a child is delinquent in hundred ways.' In reality, if a child is still alive, his mistake will affect him over time, and slow. But for example, in the recent case of a child drowning in the American River, the child died because he disobeyed his parents. When he died, that's it. No more. If he did not die, he will get into other troubles later on in life; who know what? Therefore, children is the issue of gravest concern for Vietnamese family."

If parents are expressing difficulty in coping with the contrasts between the relative openness of the new society and their traditional parental roles, children face a set of conflicting expectations and often confusing choices. In addition to such practical issues of adjustment as learning a new language, becoming accustomed to the U.S. school system, and meeting new peers, they face a host of social-psychological issues in straddling or negotiating conflicting Vietnamese values and expectations of filial respect and authority. They also must confront the expectations of independence, self-satisfaction, and questioning of authority to a point encouraged by their new society. The biggest challenge to adjustment will be for youth in carving out an identity and place in their own families and in becoming Vietnamese-American in the larger society.

A Vietnamese teacher cited the level of cultural misunderstanding that exists between recently arrived refugee families and the American school system. When a note is sent home from the teacher discussing a student's progress, it often is interpreted by the parents as a criticism of them. In the absence of government services and school and youth counseling programs to bridge these gaps, it is no wonder that many recently arrived families feel frustrated and overburdened.

The Changing Role of Women

The changing roles experienced by Southeast Asian refugee women in their new culture in which many have entered the labor market for the first time, out of choice and necessity, are leading to increased conflict and family upsets in the household. This is exacerbated by the contradictory position of the father as authority figure at home, while experiencing a loss of power in the public sphere, either by accepting a job below his skill and educational level (as is the case with first-wave Vietnamese men) or facing unemployment and discriminatory practices in the occupational world.

All of the community development specialists we interviewed concurred that increased tensions in the household are being experienced as these families attempt to reconcile the traditional with changing "modern" roles in a new cultural context, as reported by one respondent "There's a lot of real frustrations for men. They are no longer able to assume that dominant role, because they are not breadwinners anymore; they aren't held in respect anymore because they don't know English and they can't get along and that is a big problem, not only between women and men, but between parents and the children. 'Oh mom and dad, you're so old fashioned. What do you know? You don't even speak English; why do I have to listen to you? . . . It's something that Americans would say their teenagers have been saying for years, but these people are not used to it. . . . They are used to the old subordination to the parents, and that is the norm, and that's what's expected and that's how they've been trained. So then it just throws them for a loop when the kids are out of control now."

Increased conflict at home is leading new Southeast Asian refugee women to engage in additional survival strategies, such as seeking help in tension-ridden or even abusive situations. The motivation of new refugee women is especially important here because the social services available in the form of counseling and battered women's shelters often are underfunded, understaffed by bilingual counselors, and lacking in familiar cultural products and basic foodstuffs, such as rice. A community development specialist described one of her cases, which illustrates the severity of family difficulties occurring in the Southeast Asian refugee community and the extreme actions engaged in by some new refugee women:

"Family problems, there are family problems; I don't know if I can say which one is the most severe. Some groups experience some types more than others; the alienation of the kids is a big problem. Some wife abuse, some child abuse. I say child abuse is probably low, but wife abuse is higher than we like to see it. . . . And a lot of times it is a real result of frustration on the part of the men who are disempowered and who are frustrated and can't control the children, can't control their wives and that's the only way they know how. . . . People are not interested in using, say, family counseling services. Women don't know, or can't use, because of language barriers or whatever, they can't use the family or the battered women resources.

"I once had a woman who called them, one lady who called here because her husband had beat her and they were living near his family which is their custom. And she didn't have any people, you know, her own relatives here. And he forbade anybody of his family to help her, so she had nobody. . . . Once we got in contact with her, we called around to the various women shelters and . . . some of them were equipped for limited English speakers and some weren't. . . . Some of them had rice in stock and some didn't. You know that kind of thing would be [a] plus. How would the woman get there? She doesn't drive. I took her because we found out about her and it was just a very, very roundabout way we even found out about her. Because she called the only people she knew . . . being a new person here, she called her family who happened to live in Wisconsin. They called Lutheran Social Services, who called us here in Sacramento, and then we happened to get in touch with her. But, see, talk about limited access, that was very roundabout, and it's only because she is very determined that she got it. I have always been thinking since then: how many other women are there who don't get or can't get help for that kind of thing?"

New immigrant survival strategies in Sacramento have been affected significantly by changing gender relations produced by the changing social relations of female employment in the new context. Thus, first-wave Vietnamese refugee women have been willing to take any jobs to reproduce the household. Despite their middle-class backgrounds, they accepted work as manicurists, nurse's aides, and restaurant and hotel workers, as well as in labor jobs. First-wave Vietnamese men, in contrast, had tended to be government officials and did not like to take positions too different from their past experience. They avoided labor jobs, preferring unemployment or governmental clerical work when available.

Similarly, the second-wave Vietnamese refugee women obtain low-skilled service or manual labor jobs to help support their families as part of a low-income, dual-earning household or while their spouses obtain education, job training, or, in many cases, face unemployment. This has become a source of conflict and tension within these Vietnamese households because wives have been able to get clerical training and find jobs that have helped to enhance their self and social esteem while husbands have lost status, both in the household and larger society.

Bui Doi Gangs

The problems of second-wave boat people in Sacramento have been compounded by cultural misunderstandings surrounding the emergence of gang activities in their neighborhoods. In 1989 and 1990, a series of extortion attempts of small Southeast Asian-owned businesses and residential home invasion robberies began in the Lemon Hill neighborhood and nearby suburbs with Vietnamese enclaves. Press accounts based on interviews with police and some of the victims paint a picture of the rise of nomadic Vietnamese *bui doi* (dirt in the wind) gangs whose members are "fearless and ice cold" youth who "have no compassion" and engage in brutal and violent practices against fellow immigrants. These were learned initially in the squalid and chaotic refugee camps of Southeast Asia and now are reconstituted and reenacted in various "Little Saigons" throughout the U.S., including Lemon Hill.

The *bui doi* gangs are fundamentally different from other ethnic gangs in California. Their practices are delocalized; they seek neither to obtain nor defend local "turf"; and they occupy an entirely new social space. Their internal structure is based on the reproduction of transnational social networks that transcend locality, community, and place. They are nomads, rather than settlers, moving nationally and even internationally from place to place where Southeast Asian refugees are concentrated, using the easy exit option of freeways and airports to escape identification and capture. Their "home," both in transit and when operating in the scattered ethnic enclaves they victimize, is the motel. They prey upon localized ethnic households, exploiting their knowledge of the general cultural understandings and misunderstandings that handicap the least adapted segments of these communities. These vagabond gangs appropriate globalized images readily available on "Kung Fu" movies and videos to glamorize the brutal tactics they use to coerce their victims.

The *bui doi* gangs in Sacramento largely are comprised of ethnically Chinese Southeast Asian refugee youth who prey upon older refugee families reluctant to contact police because they mistrust formal institutions of law enforcement and fear reprisals. The victims are chosen precisely because of their isolation from and misunderstanding of mainstream American institutions. Unfamiliar with or mistrustful of banks, many second-wave refugee families keep their life savings in cash or commodities like gold and jewelry hidden in their homes. The gang members target such households for invasion, often torturing their robbery victims to get them to reveal the hiding place of their store of capital. Once robbed in this way, the victims' cultural misunderstanding of the legal practices of bail bonding and probation leads them to assume that their assailants have bribed police officials to obtain release from jail. They thus transfer their knowledge of corrupt practices that have been common in Vietnam both before and since the fall of Saigon into a different cultural context where it is inappropriate because it reinforces their suspicion and mistrust of potentially useful institutions and impedes the ability of the legal system to try, convict, and incarcerate a basically parasitic segment of the refugee population.

Anti-Extortion Tactics

In a dramatic example of resistance to this mode of intimidation, a Chinese-Vietnamese woman refugee, the proprietor of a local Southeast Asian market, testified against a group of gang members attempting to extort $100 per day from surrounding Southeast Asian business people. In addition, she persuaded her reluctant male employees and fellow merchants to testify against the gunmen. The courageousness of her act is evidenced by the fact that her employees repeatedly were threatened at gunpoint, while another merchant was beaten brutally at gunpoint by gang members in front of his employees and customers. Moreover, invoking law enforcement authorities demonstrates a willingness to learn about, identify with, and use the formal social controls available in the new context. In the woman's own words: "Somebody had to do something. Other people in this community scratch their own backs. It's almost a custom to keep the problem to themselves and not cause trouble. Not me. I'm not going to let this go. . . . What good is it if nobody is standing up for what is right? This is America, and I'm going to do what is right in this country. What do I gain if I let them keep coming back and threatening? I'm not scared; I work too hard to give my money to someone else."

In this case, the woman storekeeper defied cultural barriers both in overcoming traditional gender role expectations, as well as past localized suspicions of authority figures. In addition, by participating in the legal system, the rights and benefits, as well as the obligations, of citizenship are being incorporated into her identity.

Unfortunately for the community, the tactics used by law enforcement officials in Sacramento to combat the recent extortions and home invasion robberies have undermined this type of legal and political incorporation, reinforcing, rather than overcoming, the reluctance of most second-wave refugees in Sacramento to use the U.S. legal system. Despite the fact that, by their own accounting, the home invasions were perpetrated by nomadic gangsters, Sacramento police officials have engaged in a series of indiscriminate searches of local Vietnamese residents during random "sweeps" of all the patrons of restaurants, clubs, pool halls, and other establishments. In a three-week period during March 1990, scores of patrons were detained, photographed, and interrogated although there was no evidence linking them to any crimes. Challenged by civil liberties advocates for ignoring the probable cause for search requirement, these sweeps were justified by law enforcement officers, who waxed enthusiastically in the local press about their effectiveness. In defending the need for the sweeps and their legality, officers used phrases like "turning up the heat," "shaking the trees," and "putting on the pressure" in reference to the raids. Despite this implicitly intimidating rhetoric, detectives in charge of the robbery investigations told the *Sacramento Bee* that the purpose of the raids was legitimate—"We did not do this for intimidation, but for identification and intelligence gathering."

Some segments of the first-wave Vietnamese refugee community defended these raids. For example, Hung Le, an administrative aide to Sacramento Assemblyman Phillip Isenberg, blithely minimized the civil liberties violations and stigmatizing effects of the raids by telling the press: "Personally, I don't think [the raids] violated their civil rights. Hey, compared to Vietnam it's nothing. I feel those actions are necessary. It doesn't sound like democracy, but hell, it works."

Needless to say, such strategies are unlikely to reduce the mistrust of law enforcement agencies that enables the *bui doi* to operate. Indeed, they depend on precisely such mistrust. The tactics and their defense by more privileged first-wave refugees reinforce the mistrust and hence the vulnerability of the most isolated second-wave families facing the pressures of adjustment.

Complex Differences Within Communities

In America's popular understanding of the new immigration from Southeast Asia, images and representations of refugees from Vietnam have been fraught with misunder-standings, exaggerations, and sometimes even clear misrep-resentations of the fluid, highly differentiated, and still emergent character of their settlement experiences. At present, we are witnessing an emergent climate of backlash against many of America's new minorities. What some have called "the politics of difference" exists as much within as between new immigrant groups in their relations with each other and their new society. The shapers of public expec-tations of receptivity or opposition to the new minorities often fail to give due recognition to the complexity of these internal differences, thus contributing to the development of new ethnic and racial stereotypes. By paying close atten-tion to the differences within the U.S.'s newer minorities, we may be able to avoid another round of ethnic and racial antagonism in which our deep-seated structural problems are blamed on new immigrants.

Native Hostility Toward the Vietnamese

Robert Lindsey

Many Vietnamese who located in California and Texas in the 1970s and 1980s worked for the fishing industry. Some native fishermen complained that the influx of Vietnamese threatened to destroy their livelihoods. Hostilities increased to the point where violence between fishermen garnered national media attention. After the death of a white fisherman in Seadrift, Texas, the Ku Klux Klan (KKK) held anti-Vietnamese rallies, and several Vietnamese crabbing boats were destroyed. In Texas and California white fishermen shot at Vietnamese vessels.

The bitterness felt toward the Vietnamese by the general public is described in this 1982 article reflecting the virulent attitudes held by residents of the Monterey Bay fishing port town of Moss Landing, California. Residents describe the refugees as greedy, amoral, and parasitic. Robert Lindsey is a best-selling author and former director of the *New York Times*'s Western News Operations.

Henry McMasters climbed aboard his salmon boat, the *Soko*, and glared at the two Vietnamese fishermen sewing their nets in a boat in an adjoining berth at this fishing hamlet [Moss Landing] on Monterey Bay [in California].

"Look at 'em," he said. "First they cleaned out the fish in their own country and now they come here and try to wipe out what we've got. We can't compete with them; they have a lower life style."

"I say, send 'em home," said Mike Bliesener, skipper of the *Charlie 1*, who had stopped by for a visit. The anger runs deep in this northern California fishing port, and state officials say it appears to reflect a growing resentment in California toward the state's population of more than 150,000 Indochinese refugees that, they say, is related at least in part to the national economic slump.

This week [July 8, 1982] Gov. Edmund G. Brown Jr. signed a bill outlawing in waters less than 60 feet deep [the use of gill nets,] a type of net used by most Vietnamese fishermen along the northern California coast that state officials contend has been responsible for the deaths of more than 20,000 migratory birds and possibly dozens of sea lions, seals, otters and other sea mammals.

Refugees Not Welcome

In Los Angeles, representatives of the State Employment Development Division say they are receiving increasing numbers of complaints from unemployed Californians about the jobs held by Southeast Asians, while some county social workers say they are hearing complaints that many of the unemployed refugees are receiving welfare assistance.

In Sacramento, an organization of homeowners recently asked a local grand jury to investigate the possibility of establishing internment camps for Vietnamese refugees. The organization asserted that the refugees were stealing and eating pets in their neighborhood, that they were living off public welfare and driving uninsured automobiles and that "almost every female refugee 14 years of age or older is either pregnant or has been pregnant."

There are indications that the welcome mat accorded Southeast Asian refugees is wearing thin elsewhere, too. Sister Ann Wisda, head of the United States Catholic Conference of Oklahoma, which has aided about 5,000 Vietnamese refugees since North Vietnam overran Saigon in 1975, told an Oklahoma newspaper . . . that many had become "parasites" and that some newly arrived refugees asked "when they'll receive their first welfare check and food stamps as soon as they leave the plane."

On April 1 [1982], the Reagan Administration reduced to 18 months, from 36 months, the length of time that the Federal Government grants cash assistance, of up to $248 a month, and free medical care to refugees. The state has been promised additional stopgap assistance to continue limited help to its large population of refugees, but social welfare agencies have been warning in recent weeks that the refugees are likely to be an increasingly heavy financial burden for some counties at a time when local government in California is already experiencing a serious financial squeeze.

Rough Times

Spokesmen for the Vietnamese in California say they are growing concerned by what some regard as the emergence of racial bias toward the refugees.

"I personally feel that it's mostly because of economic factors," said Duong Bui, an instructor at the Defense Language Institute at nearby Fort Ord. But he said another factor was the changing nature of Vietnamese immigrants.

"In the past, we had well-to-do, educated people," he said. "We have a new group now who are not as educated, and they are competing for blue-collar jobs."

Mai Dao, who teaches a class at San Jose State University designed to acquaint public officials, social workers and others with Vietnamese culture and language, said tensions between refugees and non-Vietnamese were growing principally because "these are just rough times."

"Remember, these are people who had to escape," she said. "They have nothing left. They are starting a new life. They have to have drive to survive. They are not sitting back. They are working hard for their children.

'That makes for envy," she said. "People say that the Vietnamese will do anything. Well, they will, they are rough competitors because they are trying to survive."

At Moss Landing, there seems to be an invisible barrier between American fishermen and the Vietnamese who operate 22 small pleasure boats that have been outfitted with tall masts that they have used to lay down gill nets, made of thin filaments of nylon a mile or more in length.

Mr. Bui, who has served as a spokesman for the Vietnamese fishermen, said that they did not understand and were "stunned" by the new legislation.

As aliens, they were already forbidden to use large commercal fishing boats, and now they will be unable to fish for kingfish. The shallow-water fish was long considered unappealing to American fishermen, but the Vietnamese have caught and sold it, mostly to the state's Oriental population, for about 25 cents a pound.

"So Damn Greedy"

Unlike a confrontation between Vietnamese and American fishermen in Galveston Bay in Texas, there has not been any violence between the two groups here.

But at Teri's, the coffeeshop where they congregate, and along the wharf, a dozen American fishermen interviewed at random all spoke with the same intensity about the Vietnamese.

"They're so damn greedy," said one, Larry Clark. "They get all that help from the Government that comes from our taxes. With this depression, the price of fish is down. I'll tell you one thing: This thing between us and the Vietnamese is going to get a lot worse."

"They fish for anything," said Don Dorr, skipper of the *Meridian*. "They use these nets that get sea lions and salmon and when they lose the nets, it sours the area for years. The nylon doesn't deteriorate, and for years they stay there and trap fish and kill 'em."

The Lost Investment

Nearby, Xa Van Nguyen, who came from Vietnam two years ago and invested everything his family had in a small pleasure craft now outfitted with a $5,000 gill net, worked silently on the rigging of his boat, trying to ignore a group of American fishermen looking over at him.

Several of the Americans were shouting their disapproval of the Vietnamese so loudly that it seemed impossible for him to ignore their voices. But he kept his head down and continued to work.

A few minutes later they were gone, and a visitor to his boat asked what he planned to do now that use of gill nets had been restricted. He looked up and smiled and said, "I don't know."

CHAPTER 3

Later Waves Up to the Present Day

COMING TO AMERICA

Little Saigon

Stanley Karnow

In this selection Stanley Karnow, a journalist and author
who has written extensively on Vietnam, profiles the flour-
ishing Vietnamese American community of Little Saigon
in Orange County, California. He describes a diverse community that offers a unique insight into Vietnamese culture. He also discusses how many residents of Little Saigon
struggle to adjust to a new society. Karnow points out that
organizations in Little Saigon serve the important function
of providing support for a community of survivors.

Thousands of immigrants from Southeast Asia are now re-
building their lives in Southern California, but the going
is not always easy.

"Americans go to bank for loan, Vietnamese go to
friends," Gi is saying. "I ask this guy for a thousand, another for two thousand, soon I have eighteen thousand. We
trust each other, so no interest. He know I do the same for
him one day."

Nguyen Huu Gi, a slender and amiable man, is explaining how he was able to start the little computer store that
he runs with his family in a part of California that, for his
visitor, resonates with echoes of another time and another
country.

When I left Vietnam after years of covering the war, I
never expected to see Saigon again. But I am back there
now, at least in spirit. For the Vietnamese refugees who

have streamed into California since the Communists conquered their country in 1975 have created a facsimile Saigon in Orange County, an hour's drive south of Los Angeles. To commemorate its antecedents—and in hopes of diverting tourists from nearby Disneyland—the local authorities have formally recognized the area's character in a freeway sign: "Little Saigon."

Support for Survivors

Insecure on alien soil, newcomers have historically clung together during their early years in America. Irish congregated in Boston, Germans in Milwaukee, the Jews and Italians in New York City. But the Vietnamese feel an even stronger urge to cluster. Unlike immigrants, who uprooted themselves by choice, they are refugees from war, devastation and political repression, and many continue to be traumatized by their perilous escapes. They are also tormented by an almost obsessive nostalgia for a native land that, many fear, they may never see again. Though most have shown extraordinary resilience, others have failed to adjust fully to America, and their problems are straining their mental stability as well as their family lives. As a Vietnamese social worker explained to me, "We are survivors, grasping each other for support. A place like Little Saigon provides that support."

The U.S. Government, striving to avert a repetition of the massive Cuban impact on Miami, originally attempted to disperse the first Vietnamese arrivals around the country. The policy miscarried.

Seeking to be with their relatives and friends, and lured by a warm climate reminiscent of home, more than a quarter of the one million Vietnamese refugees who poured into America after 1975 eventually migrated to California. At least 70,000 settled in Orange County, making it the biggest concentration of Vietnamese outside Vietnam.

If Vietnam meets America in Little Saigon, it is also where the two cultures collide. Scanning the Orange County telephone directory, for example, I encounter pages of Nguyens and Phams, the Vietnamese parallels of Smith and Jones. But many have adopted such American first names as Harry and Pat. Those who have kept their Vietnamese names often reverse them in Western fashion, so that a friend of mine, formerly Tran Nghia, is now Nghia Tran. East and West blend in enterprises like the Eurasian Mortgage Company.

Vietnamese Shopping Centers

Little Saigon is devoted to commerce, as its prototype was before the Communists curbed capitalism. But while the refugees have transplanted their own brand of business in this foreign setting, they have embraced the most American of consumer institutions—the shopping center.

The towns of Garden Grove, Westminster and Santa Ana, which form the core of the Orange County Vietnamese community, bustle with malls like the Asian Village and the Le Loi Center, the latter named for a 15th-century Vietnamese emperor, and they rival one another in vitality. Westminster's business district is the area formally known as Little Saigon. There one afternoon, cruising down Bolsa Avenue, a main artery, I stop at the Asian Garden, an ornate two-story arcade whose curved tile roof and lacquered pillars were designed to evoke the Orient. At its entrance sits a mammoth Buddha flanked by the gods of prosperity, longevity and happiness, a quartet presumably convened to inspire confidence in its merchandise. Stepping inside, I am propelled into what the real Saigon might be today had America and its South Vietnamese clients won the war.

Blaring from audio-cassette stores is a cacophony of music ranging from hard rock to syrupy sentimental, all in Vietnamese. Peering into one, I see tapes made in Vietnam, legal through an amendment to the U.S. embargo on trading with the former enemy. There are travel agencies that primarily ticket Vietnamese, who are increasingly returning to Vietnam on visits. "Homesickness," a Vietnamese editor told me, "is reaching epidemic proportions here."

The arcade abounds in jewelers, testimony to the Vietnamese propensity to convert savings into gems or gold rather than trust the banks. A pharmacy contains, instead of aspirin and cold pills, drawers of such esoteric items as ground antler, dried lizard, starfish flakes and assorted grades of ginseng, a prized restorative that can cost as much as $2,000 a pound. I browse through bookshops stocked with novels, political tracts and girlie magazines, all published locally in Vietnamese. As in old Saigon, there are custom tailors surrounded by bolts of cloth, and dressmakers prepared to run up *ao dais*, the flowing silk tunic-and-pants ensembles worn by Vietnamese women at ceremonies. Cafes are crowded with Vietnamese men chatting over glasses of cafe au lait, just as they did in the real Saigon, where conversation was a cottage industry. The malls are also information hubs, where refugees exchange news and gossip, mainly about Vietnam. . . .

Nightlife in Little Saigon

Unlike old Saigon, a raucous wartime tenderloin of bars and nightclubs, Orange County is quiet—except on Saturday nights, when the action can be found at such discos as the Ritz, where I am taken by friends.

[In] the spacious hall . . . beams of light pierce clouds of dry-ice smoke. A Vietnamese combo called the Shotguns switches from waltzes to tangos to rock as Vietnamese couples of every age pack the floor—the women in black tights, designer jeans or frilly frocks, the men in blue denims, flashy suits or cowboy outfits. The star attraction is Lynda Trang Dai, a 24-year-old beauty billed as the "Vietnamese

Madonna," who struts in a sequined bra and hot pants as she belts out rock tunes in Vietnamese. I later learn from a newspaper interview with her that she escaped from Saigon with her family in 1978, and started singing at a California high school. Her sexy image is just a pose, she says. "I don't smoke, I don't drink. I'm just your typical Vietnamese girl." But there are no "typical" Vietnamese refugees. Many have thrived, many have lagged behind—and many languish in poverty. According to Walter Barnes, a California refugee and immigration official, "There are some tremendous successes and tremendous failures. In the middle is a bunch of people trying to do their best.". . .

Pressures of a New Society

Though they are purportedly models of harmony, many [Vietnamese families] are frustrated by the pressures of America. Numbers of refugee couples brought their difficulties from Vietnam, where wartime tensions strained marriages, and the pace of America has aggravated their troubles. Divorce among them, while rare by American standards, is rising. Husbands reduced to menial jobs or welfare often lose status in their wives' eyes. Women have also discovered freedom in America. Many are working and, to their spouses' dismay, rejecting their traditional submissive role. Marriages are further threatened as Vietnamese turn toward white American men, whom they assume to be rich and able to rescue them from hardship—and who are often charmed by their grace and beauty. As one Vietnamese tells me, "Not a week passes that an American doesn't flirt with my wife."

Meanwhile, parents, preoccupied with earning a living often lack the time and energy to pay attention to their children. Or children who have adapted rapidly to America feel estranged from parents unable to adjust as quickly. Frequently kids who have become fluent in English no longer communicate easily with parents who are comfortable only in Vietnamese. "What we're seeing," a counselor at an Orange County school observed, "is the classic immigrant experience of families drifting apart because their members can't keep up with each other in a new society."

America is especially tough on the elderly. In Vietnam they were respected in accordance with Confucian tenets, and they could mingle with contemporaries in villages or urban districts. But many, particularly in California, suffer from what Dr. Ton That Niem, an Orange County psychiatrist, terms "adjustment disorder." Unable to drive, they cannot shop or visit friends, and they sit alone at home watching television in English, which they cannot understand. Their sons and daughters are too busy to see them regularly, while their Americanized grandchildren, who often cannot speak Vietnamese, frequently snub them. Many dream of returning to Vietnam—at least to die. Or, as they euphemistically put it, "I want to go back to retire.". . .

Vietnamese High School Students

One of the liveliest days I spend in Orange County is at Saddleback High School in Santa Ana. Though Vietnamese represent only about 15 percent of the student body of some 2,800, most of it Hispanic, they are invariably the valedictorians. At the 1992 commencement, 26 of the top 33 students were Vietnamese.

Sitting in on an advanced-placement English class, I am amazed by the verve of the students, most of them Vietnamese. Led by a bouncy teacher named Chris Lammers, they read aloud from Sophocles' *Oedipus Rex*, analyzing the tragedy with eloquence and even digressing into a discussion of the Freudian Oedipus complex. Later I chat with Minh Le Tran and Kieu Oanh Nguyen Ha, both straight-A students who had fled from Vietnam with their families in the late '70s.

Minh, who hopes to become a businessman, speaks of his parents' aspirations for him. "They're really proud of me," he says. "So I have to keep improving, even if there's no room for improvement. I also feel their pressure. Just study, they say. I can't wash the dishes, mow the lawn or take a summer job. Their entire goal is to see me succeed." Similarly, Kieu Oanh says, "I know that my success is a big thing for my parents, and I sense that pressure. But it's also important to me. For example, I'm in speech contests. People look at me funny when I begin, since I'm a refugee and they expect my accent to be horrible. So I feel good when they're surprised that my English is fluent."

When I raise the question of identity, Kieu Oanh replies, "My parents made me learn to read and write Vietnamese—or at least tried to. At home we speak Vietnamese and English, but my Vietnamese isn't that great, I'm more comfortable in English. I think in English. So I guess I'm not really Vietnamese but more American—maybe a kind of transitional Vietnamese."

Striving to preserve their heritage, a Buddhist center in Orange County conducts courses for Vietnamese children on Sunday mornings. About 200 kids in gray shirts and blue jeans, ages 7 to 18, sit attentively around tables in the courtyard as Vietnamese instructors lecture them. The youngest are practicing tones, a basic of the Vietnamese language, while teenagers listen to talks on Vietnamese culture. However, I notice they speak English among themselves. Standing over one girl, I also observe that her loose-leaf binder contains, besides her notes in Vietnamese, a picture of Vanilla Ice, the American rap star. . . .

Exile Politics

Civic duty in Little Saigon is organized but very separate from the larger community. While few Vietnamese merchants belong to the Westminster Chamber of Commerce, the Vietnamese Chamber of Commerce is thriving. Chiefly concerned with their own interests, they are also split into various factions, a division reflected in the dozens of flimsy Vietnamese-language journals that represent one group or another. As refugees, many are depressed as well by the burdens of survival, and they tend to focus on personal problems rather than on community affairs. Not a single Vietnamese sits on any of Orange County's town councils. But many indulge in "exile politics," mainly through impassioned anticommunist movements that maintain that they can promote change in Vietnam. Several Vietnamese critics of these movements have been murdered by extremists. Dr. Ton That Niem explains the appeal of these groups for numbers of refugees. 'Just as someone whose leg has been amputated insists that he can still feel his foot, they cannot accept the fact that they are cut off from their native land."

I drive to the town of Costa Mesa one afternoon for a meeting of the National United Front for the Liberation of Vietnam, whose well-dressed supporters resemble innocuous Rotarians as they listen to idealistic speeches. But the group did try to live up to its name in 1987, when its founder, Hoang Co Minh, attempted to infiltrate a platoon of commandos into Vietnam from adjacent Laos. Minh, a former South Vietnamese admiral who had worked as a house painter in Washington, reportedly died, and the unit was wiped out in the action. Five Front members have since been indicted by a federal grand jury for tax evasion and for conspiring to divert donations into a chain of noodle soup restaurants.

Little Saigon's future partly hinges on the future of Vietnam. Should the Communist regime crumble, as Communist regimes are doing everywhere, many older refugees may be tempted to return. Anticipating that prospect, some have already been investing in Saigon businesses under recent reforms that permit private ownership. But younger Vietnamese seem to be too directed toward mainstream America to go back to Vietnam, except on visits. The most ardent exponent of assimilation I hear is Minh Le Tran, the Saddleback High School student—whose views, I am told, are shared by many in his generation. "I feel shackled in Little Saigon," he says. "When I grow up, I want to live in some place like Maine, where it's not all Vietnamese, and I can play bridge with my neighbors on Thursday night."

Changing Roles in the Family

Paul James Rutledge

According to Paul James Rutledge in the following selection, Vietnamese families that have relocated to the United States face innumerable challenges. Among these are the stresses that come with adapting to the norms of a new society. For example, Vietnamese families have had to adopt different gender roles; whereas in Vietnam women worked in the home, in America they often became breadwinners. In addition, while Vietnamese parents encourage their children to succeed in their new nation, they often resent the "Americanization" of the younger generation.

Paul James Rutledge is an associate professor of anthropology at the University of Missouri at St. Louis.

The traditional Vietnamese family has faced tremendous change in gender roles, family expectations, generational perspectives, and family relationships since arriving in the United States. Families in flight are often separated from children or spouses, and in resettlement women have found themselves the head of a household, assuming responsibilities for which they may feel unqualified. The loss of economic security, social status, and self-esteem often creates depression, and the role reversals which may occur have placed stress on marriage relationships. Divorce, spouse abuse, and substance abuse have resulted in some cases, and the adjustment is proving to be very difficult for many Vietnamese refugee people.

The role of men within the family has changed drastically from the Vietnamese male perspective. In Vietnam where men generally dominated social settings, they are now living in a country which stresses gender equality. It may be argued that women were, in fact, more equal than the model set forth by Vietnamese males, and the gap between ideal behavior and everyday, or real, behavior tends to show the strong position of Vietnamese women. In Vietnam, the woman controlled domestic life, and . . . played an immensely important role in the family's solidarity. Nevertheless, the discrepancies between theory and practice notwithstanding, the independent status of women in America and the apparently weakening position of men vis-à-vis women within the home have been threatening to some refugee men. In exile, they feel that they have lost control over their cultural roots by having fled their country of origin, and now, perhaps, they are losing control over their family.

> Everything has changed here. In Vietnam, I would slap my wife and children to discipline them, . . . to let them know that I love them. Here in the United States, if I slap my wife she may call the police and I could be arrested. Our discipline has come apart [unraveled], and I think I am not in charge of my family any more. [Vietnamese elder, 53 years of age, Oklahoma City]

In Vietnam, the man, as the head of the household, was traditionally the sole provider for his family. He was not expected to assist with housework or to prepare meals. In America, where the man often has a wife who works outside the home, he is no longer the exclusive provider and is now being asked to assume a greater responsibility in domestic tasks. The authority associated with his traditional role has diminished and Vietnamese men are slowly adjusting to these new expectations. "Sometimes I cook, uh

huh," admits a Vietnamese father of seven who lives in
New Orleans. "I do the vegetables, and I help with housework when my wife is too tired. This is hard for me, but it
is okay." The perspective of this man's wife does not coin-
cide entirely with his, but the adjustment process to changing roles is seen clearly in their varying statements:

> Most of the time, my husband sits in his big chair and re-
> laxes when he comes home from work. He helps me with
> some of the housework and sometimes cooking, but he
> is not very good. This is hard for him. It is also hard for
> me. I try to show him that he is still the head of the fam-
> ily and that his helping does not change that. [Viet-
> namese mother of seven, New Orleans]

The Role of Women

The role of women within the family has changed consid-
erably in the transition to America. While retaining the
roles of wife and mother, Vietnamese refugee women have
encountered new opportunities in the United States. These
opportunities to attend school, work outside the home, and
establish an identity which includes some degree of independence from one's husband have been both a blessing
and a burden. Employment outside of the primary household has resulted in a restructuring of the family. Family
pressures to assume more traditional roles have created
some conflict, and the insecurity of some refugee males
has created tension as well.

Refugee women in the American workforce have
learned that the pressures are not limited to adjustments
at home. They face the same difficulties and problems as
other working American women, including wage and ad-
vancement discrepancies, inequities in evaluation, inadequate childcare, and insufficient pay scales. Balancing
these new challenges in the social environment with the
changes at home, refugee women are perhaps changing

more dramatically than anyone else within the family setting, and not all refugee women view the changes with the same enthusiasm.

> The new changes are good for me and for my family. I like helping pay the family expenses, and I think my husband is starting to accept this. My children like it, too, because we have more money for clothes and we are planning to buy a bigger house. [Refugee woman, Southern California]

> I like to work because I get a chance to meet more Americans and to know the city better. If I stay at home all day, I would not have anything to do. My husband works all day, and my children are in college, so it is good for me to get out of the house. [Refugee woman, Tulsa]

> I think that money independence is hurting us [Vietnamese families]. At work, women are meeting American men and some are in trouble [having affairs], even some who are married. This independence of the family is causing divorce which we did not have like this in Vietnam. I think that it is very bad. [Refugee woman, California]

> I don't know if it is good or bad. I just think that this is how we do it in America. So we will all just learn to live this way and still keep our families strong. [Refugee woman, Oklahoma City]

Among the many changes within the family, the most unacceptable to the Vietnamese community at large is that of divorce. The idea of men helping with the housework often draws snickers in a group conversation, the idea of women working outside the home is grudgingly accepted as an economic reality, but the growing number of divorces in the refugee community continues to be a source of deep concern on the part of community leaders. In Vietnam, divorce was essentially unknown, and until 1959 when polygyny was out-lawed by the Vietnamese government, a man was responsible for his wife or wives for the duration of their lives. In cases of incompatibility, it was considered far better to have a mistress, or abandon the family, than to divorce. In the United States, where divorce is socially acceptable, and where economic independence is far more accessible for both genders than in Southeast Asia, divorces have been on the rise. Figures are difficult to acquire since divorce is highly stigmatized among Vietnamese communities and because it is considered dishonorable by refugees. Local conversations, however, in Oklahoma City, Dallas, New Orleans, Kansas City, and Westminster [Calif.] indicate that Vietnamese-American Associations and other Mutual Assistance Associations have now added full time counselors to their staffs who spend considerable time working with couples considering divorce. In 1984, counseling was provided for thirty-two couples in Oklahoma City by the Indochinese Refugee Crisis Center, and in Dallas, local ministers counseled several dozen Vietnamese couples who were considering separation or divorce.

Refugee children and adolescents are also faced with changes in societal and family roles. Within American society they face the identical problems as other American youth—peer pressure, aspects of self-identity, drug and alcohol abuse—in addition to language problems and the sense of loss. Refugee young people who have entered the U.S. as young children often arrive without a parent, sibling, or extended kinsperson who was lost during the flight from Vietnam, over the sea route, or separated during the asylum-camp experience. Disorientation is common, and at a time when they need special guidance and attention, the children's parents may be as confused as the children.

Introduced into an American educational system which is new and whose expectations are initially foreign, most refugee youth work diligently to achieve success in the American system. This work ethic which aids their adaptability has proven, also, to be a two-edged sword. The more successful they are in school, the more American they are perceived to be by their parents, and although their parents are extremely proud, they are leery of the distance caused by their child's growing American identity.

> My son speaks English better [than me] and he does not speak Vietnamese good. Sometimes I have to get him for understanding [translating] and this I don't like. It makes him think he is better [than me]. [Vietnamese elder, Tết Celebration, Oklahoma]

Learning English at a more rapid pace than many of their parents, refugee children are placed in a Catch-22 position. They must learn the language to survive, but in their success they, by default, are relied upon by parents in more difficult language situations. This reliance creates a role reversal from traditional Vietnamese society, and sometimes results in conflict within the family. Consternation of the child or adolescent grows as he or she continues the attempt to live between two cultures: the Vietnamese culture of the home; the American culture of society.

Traditions in Conflict

The acceptance of a new standard by adolescents inevitably decreases the ties to historical precedents. The traditional value of obeying one's parents is not completely discarded by Vietnamese-American youth, but it is shared with outside influences and authorities. Often these influences are in conflict.

> My father tells me that I cannot smoke, but all my friends smoke. When I try to explain, he threatens to beat me. I have already made some plans, and if he tries to hurt me, I will leave. He cannot make me be like him. My father is very important to me, but lately we do not get along very well. I wish there was some way he could accept me. I am an American. I am not a Vietnamese like he is. [Vietnamese youth, sixteen years of age, Oklahoma City]

Refugee young people, who like many other American youth are at risk from illegal substances, alcohol abuse, and gang membership, are nevertheless excelling as a group in their principal endeavor: education. Maintaining the long-held value placed on education, the responsibility of children, second only to filial respect, is to achieve excellence in school. High educational performance is expected of both males and females, and following the school day, children are required to study after arriving at home. In some homes, watching television is only allowed on the weekends, and study is expected even if the teacher has not made assignments. In those cases, the parent may write questions for the child, or they may read ahead and study what they did in school during that day. The ultimate goal is a college education and graduate studies depending on the career chosen by the child in order that the child may obtain "appropriate standing" in the community. That is not to indicate, however, that all Vietnamese youth excel in their scholastic pursuits. The myth of Asian-American superiority in the classroom may be countered by those refugee youths who are average academically and who lack motivation to continue past high school. The success factor for Asian-Americans is tied to their respect for education and their tandem hard work in achieving an education, not to genetic factors or any magical abilities.

In concert with other family members who are introduced to unfamiliar customs in the social environment, Vietnamese children and young people come in contact with new behaviors and perspectives throughout their educational careers. Their response to date has been mixed; some of the new customs they readily accept, some they participate in but do not particularly adopt, and some they reject outright. They have maintained a respect for the family as a whole, and for parental leadership. They have rejected forms of extreme independence which would mandate moving outside the home, or acting out toward parents, but they have created a middle ground. They are acquiring and employing independence while retaining family ties. They are fashioning a new model of the Vietnamese-American communities of the twenty-first century.

The Vietnamese Find a Niche Doing Nails

Janet Dang

In the following selection Janet Dang reports that thousands of Vietnamese American women and their burgeoning personal care businesses have revolutionized the nail industry. The huge number of Vietnamese Americans pursuing cosmetology licenses in the state of California has precipitated changes in the way the test is given, including the offering of classes and examinations in Vietnamese. Additionally, Vietnamese men are also becoming nail technicians. Janet Dang is a reporter for *Asian Week*.

For 13 years, Kim has taken hundreds of Californians by the hand, skillfully executing a routine guaranteed to make a better impression, even if there isn't an imminent wedding or corporate meeting or important interview.

The cost: Less than $50.

Like thousands of other Vietnamese Americans, mostly women, Kim is a licensed manicurist who can, within the space of an hour or a bit longer, turn the stubby, bitten fingernails of a stressed-out worker into perfectly polished tips. As owner of Union Nails in San Francisco's Pacific Heights, that has been her business for 13 years.

Kathy Diep has achieved that dream, too. Diep, 59, has run Kathy's Nails in San Francisco's Financial District since the early '90s. Before that, she was at a swanky salon closer to Union Square frequented by celebrities. She did a great job, as a signed picture by *The Birds* actress Tippi Hedren attests.

Like other Vietnamese Americans, Diep has learned that a nurturing, friendly atmosphere goes a long way toward keeping customers. Her second-floor salon offers a stress antidote to all clientele. Want your toenails pampered, your back rubbed? Kathy's can do that. And a sympathetic ear and motherly advice are free. On one weekday, Diep buffed and polished as she dispensed some tips on smoothing over a mother-in-law relationship: "You have to love her, because without her, you wouldn't have your husband."

A Vietnamese Innovation

Such shops began proliferating in Southern California where the Vietnamese population is by far most heavily concentrated. In the '80s, Vietnamese American nail salon owners spearheaded the concept of the "discount" salon, a bare-bones, fluorescent-lit shop where a complete set of acrylic tips could be had for less than $25.

By 1998, the manicure market was worth $6.4 billion for salon services alone, up from $6.2 billion the year before, according to *Nails* magazine. Getting one's nails done didn't have to be just for wedding days or well-heeled society matrons, but became part of a routine for the working class and teenage girls, too. For example, acrylic nails— one of the most popular services—require at least bimonthly maintenance visits and have kept clients coming back, sometimes for more expensive treatments like airbrush-painted nails.

Though hard numbers aren't available, *Nails* magazine Editor in Chief Cynthia Drummey estimates that about half of the nation's manicurists are of Vietnamese descent. "There is a low barrier of entry," she said, noting that many trainees hope eventually to own a salon and the profits that go with it.

Drummey couldn't put her finger on why Vietnamese Americans are doing nails, saying only that they "have an orientation for personal care service." But nonetheless, getting hired at a place where the boss speaks your language is always easier than the converse.

Nationwide, 311,725 people are licensed as manicurists (Alaska, Utah, Connecticut and Nebraska do not require certification). More than a quarter of them live in California. With 85,260 technicians, the state's salons boast on average 12 technicians apiece, a higher ratio than any other state.

"It's a huge business for the Vietnamese," said Drummey, who said the magazine's surveys indicate far more of that ethnicity than other Asian ethnicities or races. Blacks and Latinos together make up only about 10 percent of the market, Drummey estimated, and whites and Asian Americans of other ethnicities make up the rest, she said.

"The Vietnamese salons were good for the industry," Drummey said. "They brought down the prices and expanded the market of potential customers."

Certification in Vietnamese

Becoming a nail technician is not easy. In California, 400 hours of training (about 10 weeks at beauty schools) are required to secure a license. Nor is it cheap. Ten weeks of tuition at Evergreen Beauty College in San Jose costs $850, according to the school's director, licensed cosmetologist Sophia Tran.

The nail industry has become so pervasive among Asian immigrants, especially Vietnamese, that even cosmetology certification tests in California are administered in three different languages: Vietnamese, Japanese and Spanish.

And the clientele continues to grow. Students range anywhere between ages 17 (the minimum age requirement) to over 50. About 80 percent are of Vietnamese descent,

Tran said. Because of the mix, she said, classes are taught in two languages—English and Vietnamese.

The director said she thinks Asian Americans, particularly Vietnamese, have a knack for the job. "I think the skill, you know, the Asian people they have the skill to do nails. They do a very good job. American women say Vietnamese women do nails very good. And it's easy."

Tran said teaching in two languages ensures that more students will grasp the material. "We take more time to teach our students," Tran said. "American students—they're not happy. . . . They have to wait."

Still, becoming a nail technician requires more than a knack for details. Before applying artificial nails, manicurists must buff and file natural nails and trim cuticles with instruments that can cause infection if unsterile. Then, they concoct and apply eye-watering acrylic pastes and glues to natural nails, taking care to avoid inhaling noxious powders and fumes. Removing cracked tips—which commonly occur after more than a week of wearing false tips, means pulling and cutting the acrylic facade off with sharp instruments. If incorrectly done, the procedure can imperil or even destroy natural fingernails.

Smear Tactics

Though problems do occur, some in the industry suspect ritzy salons of starting a race-tinged hysteria about hygiene in the Vietnamese American salons.

"Some of the high-end salons were threatened. And sometimes it was racially tinged," Drummey acknowledged. "There was a lot of animosity that was directed at a lot of the Vietnamese salons, and that's unfortunate."

In February [1999], Los Angeles TV station KCBS aired an investigative report on the health risks of nail salons in the area, most of which are owned by Asian Americans.

"They are everywhere: nail salons, many offering bargain prices. But are they safe?" stated the report by Kyra Phillips. Undercover "agents" visited 16 nail salons to find only five of them had been inspected within the past three years. At one salon they observed, said the report, a manicurist was caught "eating with her fingers. Without washing her hands, she began working on the agent's hands while still chewing her dinner. The [investigative] team learned that that same manicurist was also not licensed to do nails." Later, another employee was seen using a microwave oven, "to heat up chemicals for a waxing job—the same oven used to heat the first manicurist's food. . . . "

At no point, though, did Phillips say that any client had lost a finger or a hand or a life to a bad nail job. Efforts to interview the California Department of Health Services about this topic were unsuccessful.

A Lucrative Endeavor for Both Sexes

"Some students are very successful. Make money a lot," Tran said. "It's up to them if they work hard, practice a lot—they can make money."

But most manicurists face years of waiting before they have a chance at earning top salaries. Even after that, most manicurists spend years as independent contractors, renting salon booths for $100 to $200 a month. "You pay a flat fee; you keep all the money while you work out of the salon," explained Drummey.

On average, manicurists who don't own their own salon can make a living, though not a luxurious one. According to *Nails* magazine, the average take home pay for a technician in 1998 was $469.24 a week including tips, down from $482 in 1997. A salon manager or owner made on average $553 per week.

Kim has seen her clientele list grow beyond female professionals, encompassing a growing number of teenage girls and in recent years, men. In fact, she said, her 26-

year-old son has a nail certificate, and owns Union Nails No. 2 downtown.

Men get paid on average $713 per week, over 60 percent more than their female counterparts' $443.

If statistics at Evergreen Beauty College are any indication, the word is out. About 20 percent of the students at the Evergreen Beauty College in San Jose are men, according to director Tran. "They're very good," she said.

Still, men account for only 2.4 percent of licensed manicurists nationwide, according to *Nails* magazine. Among them is Vietnamese American David Hoang, a licensed manicurist for nine years who manages five other technicians at Nails 2007 in Bradenton, Fla. He has placed first in national competitions at least three times, bringing home upwards of $1,000 cash prizes each time for nail art and nail sculpture. This year, Hoang notes, he entered about a dozen competitions.

In Vietnam, recalled the 34-year-old, he painted countryside landscapes and portraits. Now he paints nails—and though the canvas is often less than thumbnail-sized, the artistic task remains challenging.

Hoang, who worked as a computer programmer for two years before his company downsized, said his job as a nail technician offers him both creativity and security—as well as the prospect of making $1,000 a week or more.

"Nobody's gonna lay me off," he said. "Its a very demanding industry." The best part about his job, he added, is "making friends."

Unlike Hoang, many male manicurists are decidedly low-profile. While all the female manicurists interviewed declined to have their pictures taken, only Hoang consented to an interview.

For many men, cosmetology is a second job or a track to owning their own business, according to Tran. Like Hoang, many men are drawn in by relatives. With most dis-

count salons owned by families, husbands, brothers and
sons sometimes decide to get licenses and help out.

"More men are in the business; more Vietnamese are
defying the stereotype," Drummey noted. "I don't think
there's quite a stigma attached anymore," she said. "We
ought to recruit more men."

The Role of Language

But there are signs that California has reached a saturation
point. Hoang himself used to live in that state, but moved
to Florida to make a better living. Others, he noted, have
moved to Texas or Maryland, Chicago or Miami.

Why don't they do something else? Language has a lot
to do with it, Hoang said. "Many Vietnamese, when they
came here to America, they did not have background or
education," he said. Or "they are looking, the easiest to
find a job is doing nails."

The relative lack of status and the hard work involved
may mean that the trend started by Vietnamese immigrants 20 years ago may have peaked for that group. Even
Drummey says she's noticed a change. Vietnamese immigrants' children, she said, "are acclimated to the American life and are not willing to work under the same condition." Nevertheless, Drummey doubts the Vietnamese
segment of the market is going to disappear. "The Vietnamese salons aren't going anywhere," she said.

To that effect, Kim seems to agree. Buffing nails and
applying polish all day is not a fascinating nor a glamorous
job, she maintains. But with limited English and education, she has concluded that it's what she wants to do.

"The younger people, they go to school and learn English. They don't want to do nails. They work in offices."

A Young Vietnamese American Explores His Roots in Vietnam

Alys Willman

Duy Tan Nguyen, a young Vietnamese American film-maker based in Louisville, Kentucky, experienced a cultural awakening after viewing a video he received in the mail of his great grandfather's funeral, which took place in Vietnam. He decided to travel to Vietnam to meet relatives whom he had never seen. Nguyen, with his camcorder in tow, decided to document his trip for a film school project, even though he knew it would be difficult to smuggle the film past Communist Vietnamese censors on his way out of Vietnam. In the following selection Alys Willman describes Nguyen's trip back to Vietnam and the emotions he experienced during and after his trip. Although the young filmmaker enjoyed his experience in Vietnam, Willman reports, he is grateful to have been raised in the United States. Duy Tan Nguyen continues to work in the motion picture industry; his most recent projects include visual effect work on *Looney Tunes: Back in Action* and *The Day After Tomorrow*. Journalist and editor Alys Willman currently resides in Chile.

Three years ago, 23-year-old amateur filmmaker Duy Tan Nguyen popped a video into his VCR in Louisville and watched his great-grandfather die 8,500 miles away.

The video, sent by friends in Nguyen's native village of

Alys Willman, "The Vietnamization of Duy Tan Nguyen," *Louisville Magazine*, vol. 47, December 1996, p. 40. Copyright © 1996 by Alys Willman. Reproduced by permission.

Phuoc Thinh, Vietnam, spanned the last two weeks of the old man's life as friends and family visited to pay their last respects and a priest administered last rites. Nguyen's grandfather stood next to the bed, fanning his beloved progenitor.

Then the entire village formed a death procession from the leaning house of the dead man to the cemetery. Hundreds of villagers, all ages, all dressed in ceremonial high-collared white shirts and dark pants, followed the coffin-bearers as they wound their way through the dusty streets to the burial site.

The scene stirred memories that years of Americanization had blotted out. On his video screen were a great-grandfather and grandfather he had never known, and a village and life he could not remember.

Full of questions about his Vietnamese heritage and family, and determined to meet his grandfather before he, too, passed away, Nguyen (his full name is pronounced "Zree Tahn Gwen") began planning to go back to Vietnam. This past February [1996] he went, bringing a borrowed camcorder.

The documentary he filmed about his experiences there not only put him in touch with his native culture and family, but won him a prestigious travel grant as he graduated from college. To fulfill his mission, though, he had to smuggle controversial video footage past strict Vietnamese authorities—not an easy task.

A Family Scattered

Born near the end of the Vietnam war, Nguyen immigrated to the U.S. with his parents, older brother, both grandmothers, and an aunt and uncle when he was two years old. Thinking the trip was temporary, Nguyen's grandfather and great-aunt stayed behind to take care of the family property in Vietnam.

After a brief cultural orientation in Guam, the passel of Nguyens set sail for California, where they stayed a few months before heading eventually to New Orleans. The family began to scatter as members stayed behind in both places.

When Duy was seven, he moved with his parents, older brother and new younger brother and sister to Louisville, where his parents found work in a packaging factory.

Living in the Buechel area, the boy confronted a daily contrast of going to a predominantly white school, then coming home to a white neighborhood and a vastly different Vietnamese household. "I was always the only Asian anywhere I went," he says. "I spent eight years in private Catholic grade school and high school (St. Xavier), and if that's not enough to help a kid lose his language and want to be white, I don't know what is."

As with other children of immigrants, the gap between family heritage and American culture widened as he got older. "We all grew up resenting our parents a lot. We thought, why can't they do what the other parents can do? Why can't they speak English like everyone else does? . . . And it was hard to be able to talk to my parents about the things I was thinking about."

His parents struggled to keep their children connected with Vietnamese customs and values, but the forces of society were often stronger. "They tried to keep things at home Vietnamese, but they worked all sorts of odd hours," Nguyen says. "When we came home from school, they were leaving for work."

And though he knew all about the Renaissance and the Middle Ages, he wasn't learning much about his Asian background at school. "I think every minority will agree," he says, "living in this country you're taught European history. Where does Asia apply to all that? When you're taught like that, you think those are the important events, but there's billions of people adjacent to that continent with thousands of years of history. How come I didn't learn about that? You think maybe it doesn't matter. It makes you feel negative about your own culture."

Nguyen's only exposure to Vietnamese history in school was the American perspective, and that was limited to a short chapter on the Vietnam War, and the opinions of others. "I ran into a lot of Vietnam vets, usually at bus stops, and as soon as they looked at me they'd start talking about the war," he says. "So I'm not a person; I'm just a reminder of a war."

It wasn't until his teenage years that Nguyen came into contact with other Vietnamese immigrants in Louisville. "I didn't really know there was a Vietnamese community in Louisville till I was older," he says. "We went to a Christmas mass in the Vietnamese community. I was totally shocked."

His surprise at seeing others like himself inspired questions about his own place in American culture. "I thought, why am I so shocked to go to a Vietnamese mass and see people with black hair and a tan when I have all those characteristics?" he says. "When I feel more comfortable around white people, what's going on here?"

At 18, Nguyen left Louisville for Cleveland on a scholarship to the Cleveland Art Institute. He majored in photography, dabbled in film, and eventually developed an interest in cross-cultural experiences and filmmaking. He also met more young people of Asian descent, which piqued his interest in his native culture a little more.

Am I American or Vietnamese?

The combination of his great-grandfather's death and the 20th anniversary of the end of the Vietnam war in 1995 prompted more questions about his heritage. The time seemed right to make a documentary about his Vietnamese heritage and adapting to the United States. "Vietnam was in the news and the doors were opening for other countries. . . . I thought I'd better start doing something because I felt a little left out of this picture, considering my background is Vietnamese and I had a lot of questions about it," he says. "And I was making decisions about whether or not I wanted to keep up with the culture my parents handed to me. I was battling in my head as to whether I was American or Vietnamese."

Nguyen wrote a proposal for his documentary project and began looking for sponsors for his trip. A local church gave him money for a plane ticket, and friends and family loaned him camera equipment.

In February of [1996], Nguyen stepped off a plane in Ho Chi Minh City (formerly Saigon) with his borrowed camera equipment to spend a month at his great-aunt's house there. His worries about fitting in, if he had any, dissolved quickly. "I felt totally at home," he says. "After the first day I was walking around half-naked, sleeping in the same bed with everyone else, and everyone treated me like they'd known me their whole lives."

Looking a little more sophisticated than the average tourist, with two large camera bags hung on each arm, a tripod and other pieces of equipment, Nguyen had no trouble finding things to shoot. Street markets, cluttered narrow alleyways, and Vietnamese chatter echoed everywhere, as villagers haggled for the ripest fruit and children jumped excitedly in front of the camera, begging to be on film. Other villagers offered to take him inside shops, on mopeds through the chaos of traffic, or into the clubs and brothels that lined the streets.

But as eager as they were to be on film, the Vietnamese were less than willing to answer the questions Nguyen asked. "They'd basically talk about the weather, and how nice the city is, and how things are getting better," he recalls. "But there were no names, like who's doing stuff to make it better. Nobody would complain about education or quality of living, or whatever." Nobody, that is, except Sang Wirick, another Vietnamese-American visiting his home country, whom Nguyen had met on the plane. Wirick had emigrated when he was 12 in 1974, and was old enough to remember Vietnam during the war. After living in San Diego for 20 years, he had learned to speak his mind.

In a two-hour interview, Wirick spoke candidly about the problems of poverty, prostitution and government corruption in Vietnam. Those sentiments, combined with a smattering of street scenes and other footage, gave Nguyen everything he needed for a prizewinning documentary. Unfortunately, the Vietnam authorities disagreed.

According to Vietnam policy, every videotape made during a visit must be submitted to the authorities for inspection three days before the tourist leaves the country. A friend of Wirick's was supposed to help get Nguyen's tapes past inspection, but those plans fell through. "Connections are the way to survive in Vietnam," the filmmaker says. "Everything's done under the table. We tried to get this friend to slip the tapes by, but it didn't work out, and they ended up seeing the tapes."

A Setback

Because of the controversial content of the Wirick interview, the government was now pretty curious about just what this American kid was doing with all his fancy equipment. All of Nguyen's tapes were confiscated.

But fate was smiling on him. During the three-day interim when the authorities were inspecting the tapes, Nguyen managed to track down his long-lost grandfather in Phuoc Thinh. His last contact with his grandfather had been in 1975, when he carried two-year-old Duy to the boat as the Nguyens left Vietnam.

The 72-year-old man rode two and a half hours under

tropical sun on a rusty moped to see his grandson and take him to the village where he was born.

"He's a total goofball," Duy says. "I really like him. My 72-year-old grandfather was out running around, swimming and drinking beer."

During his visit, Duy and his video camera visited his great-grandfather's grave and the house where Duy was born, now occupied by the Nguyens' former neighbors.

By the time Duy returned to Saigon, he had less than 24 hours until his plane left, not enough time to submit his newest tape to the authorities. The tape was a high-8 model, about the size of a standard audio cassette tape, and small enough to hide, he thought. But doing so meant risking detainment at the airport and enduring a lot of questions from some perturbed guards. He decided to try it anyway.

"I had the tape in my socks," he says. "When I got up to the gate, just before I got on the plane, there was a guy who had to search me. This is where I was really sweating it." Standing with his arms spread wide while the guard frisked him, Nguyen tried to distract the guard with a little humor. "I was cracking jokes with him, trying to make it laid-back, like I'm just a stupid kid . . . "

The guard stopped his search just shy of Nguyen's ankle, and the tape made it on board safely. Once back in the States, he had very little time to edit the smuggled footage for his senior project. He mailed a tape, microphone and a list of questions to Sang Wirick in San Diego, asking him to refilm the interview for his documentary, since the original had been confiscated. Using a digital editing system borrowed from a teacher friend, Nguyen put together, in three short weeks, a documentary that won him the $4,500 Gund Award, one of three top prizes given by the Cleveland Art Institute to graduating seniors. He's since sent tapes of his documentary to PBS, and has landed a job with a prominent Chicago film company.

He's also put some of the difficult questions about his culture to rest. Meeting his grandfather again and spending time in his native culture helped to resolve some of the confusion Nguyen had felt in the States. "I always saw Vietnam as one big lump," he says. "The stereotype that Asians are all the same was one I always hated, but to some extent it was in my own mind too. But to see my country as its own country, with its diversities and its problems, was good. . . . I felt at home in a way I haven't felt anywhere."

As much as he felt at home there, though, Nguyen insists that the United States is where he'll stay. Through the combination of years of questioning his identity and the month-long visit to Vietnam, he has accepted and integrated his heritage into his life in American society. The majority of his friends he met in college are Asian-American, as is his girlfriend. For Nguyen, the visit was only one step in a larger journey toward finding a place in the United States. "I guess the main question is, what am I?" he says. "I'm out to find a specific definition, or at least find what definitions are out there and how I fit into those. Am I Vietnamese, American, or Vietnamese-American?"

Right now, he's not sure. "About four generations from now, that's when my family is going to be defined as American," he says. "In a few generations when my family has a history here, then I think the definition of being American applies a lot more."

The Final Project

The film opens with several Vietnamese telling stories about their odysseys to the United States—stories of miscarried babies and crowded boats, and of the hopeless feeling that they might be leaving their families and homeland forever. Other, younger Asian-Americans tell of growing up ashamed of their dark skin and hair, of wanting to be white. They talk about dating across cultures, and trying to relate to parents across a cultural gap. Duy Tan Nguyen's friend Sang Wirick tells of moving to the States right in the critical years of childhood, at age 12, then discovering in his late 20s that not only was his father alive in Vietnam, but that he had seven sisters and two brothers there also.

Viewers meet Nguyen's great-aunt, weathered and smiling as she gathers breakfast dishes from the porch, and his spry old grandpa, who grins and offers his grandchild a beer or two in his tiny home.

In between blurred shots of Ho Chi Minh City bicycle and moped traffic and street scenes, Nguyen recounts offers of sex for $6 from pre-adolescent girls, and tells of learning, too late, that his sumptuous dinner had once wagged its tail and barked.

The title of the film, *Viet Kieu*, means "Overseas Vietnamese," a term the nation's people use to describe those who emigrate to other countries. The idea came from a conversation with his great-aunt, who asked him if he were going to marry a Vietnamese girl. Duy said he didn't think so. "Why not?" she said. "You're Vietnamese."

He replied that he thought he was "more American than anything." "You're not American," she said. "You're Viet Kieu. Overseas Vietnamese."

The last section of the documentary features Nguyen's grandfather in the same listing, crumbling house his grandson's parents grew up in, the front of which has been rented and turned into a beauty salon.

"It's now March 1996, and that makes it almost 21 years our family has been spread so far apart and things have been so mixed up," the elder Nguyen says in Vietnamese. "We never really know how each other is doing. . . . And now my grandson Duy has come home." Then his leathery face softens as he addresses his family in the States. "If you find time, please try and come back."

Vietnamese Gangs in the United States

Patrick Du Phuoc Long, with Laura Ricard

Vietnamese gangs such as the "Asian Boys," the "Oriental Boyz," or AWA (Asians with Attitudes) have grown in number and sophistication over the past fifteen years. The author of this selection, a juvenile counselor in California, argues that many Vietnamese boys feel alienated both at home and in the American educational system, and he believes this contributes to a sense of despair. Despair, in turn, leads to gang involvement as a means to achieve a sense of belonging. He warns that greater numbers of people will be affected by Vietnamese gang violence if this serious social problem is not addressed. Patrick Du Phuoc Long wrote, with Laura Ricard, a freelance journalist, *The Dream Shattered: Vietnamese Gangs in America*, from which this selection was taken.

[In 1975] with four sons and two daughters, Bim Nguyen, an ARVN (Army of the Republic of Vietnam) soldier for twenty years, and his wife, Sao, fled Vietnam aboard a small fishing boat with fifty-one other refugees. Resettled in California, sixteen years after their exodus from Vietnam, the Nguyens were quietly watching television in the small living room of their Sacramento home when an unimaginable drama unfolded before them and thousands of other viewers.

That drama featured their children. The faces of three

of their sons and a fourth assailant, a young man named Tran, flashed on the TV screen. The four had stormed into the Good Guys electronics store in South Sacramento, where they had taken forty-one hostages and were terrorizing them.

The Nguyens hastened to the scene. Sao, her cousin, and a Buddhist priest begged to talk to the boys, but police said that the gunmen would not communicate with them. "If they had let me talk to my son, Pham, I could have talked him out of it, to lay down their weapons," the mother said through an interpreter. Eight hours later, a SWAT team shot and killed two of the Nguyen children and seriously wounded the third—but not before the four had killed two store employees and a customer. Police charged the surviving twenty-one-year-old Nguyen brother with fifty-four felony counts ranging from kidnapping and assault to murder as he lay in his hospital bed.

In the aftermath of the murders, Sao Nguyen told reporters how her sons had helped around the house, and neighbors said that nothing in their behavior had suggested they would be capable of such an attack. In fact, that very morning the boys had asked their father for permission to go fishing. A Catholic priest informed reporters that the boys attended Mass every Sunday, and that one of them was an altar boy. "I'd never imagine. Never," Father Nguyen (of no relation to the family) said.

And yet, after the four gunmen allowed two groups of hostages to leave the store (these included five toddlers and their mothers), their behavior toward the remaining hostages was unimaginably cruel. They tied their hostages up with speaker wire and forced them to crawl and kneel. They pointed their weapons at the hostages' heads and swore that they were about to fire. At one point they proposed a "game": they divided the hostages into two groups, then one of the attackers flipped a coin onto the floor, indicating that those hostages on the side toward which the coin rolled would be executed first. "Let's shoot at one of his legs first to show that we mean business," one said, and one of the brothers aimed his gun at a hostage and shot him in the thigh. At nightfall, a seventy-four year-old man had a diabetic seizure; one of the gunmen shot him in the leg and warned that next time he'd shoot him in the head. A terrified pregnant woman suffered a miscarriage. Wanting to know the time, one of the assailants yanked a wristwatch from a hostage, saying, "We have no intention of ripping off your watch." Then he grabbed a fistful of bills from the register and threw them to him saying, "So we can call it even, keep the change. No problem."

On several occasions the gunmen asked for forty 1000-year-old ginseng roots (a Chinese herb valued for its medicinal properties), four "Robo-Cop" protective suits, bulletproof vests, one million dollars, a helicopter capable of carrying forty people, a .45 caliber pistol and plane tickets to Thailand to fight the Viet Cong (communist guerrillas). "Look there, we are going to be movie stars!" one assailant shouted to another when their pictures appeared on the closed-circuit TV.

Gaining access to the crawl space between the store's roof and ceiling through an adjacent shop, seven SWAT team members stole down both sides of the store just as at least two of the gunmen began to fire on the hostages. But in seconds it was over. "We have four bad guys," a SWAT marksman announced.

Movie stars indeed.

White-Collar Crime and Gangs

Unlike . . . the three Vietnamese gunmen mowed down inside a South Sacramento electronics store, another criminal—let's call him Danny—came to America from Vietnam with several advantages. Arriving in 1975 when Saigon fell to the communists, he was armed with a high school degree, money, some knowledge of English, and, having lived on the border of Saigon's Chinatown, many friends among Chinese businessmen. This last he might have used to great profit. But Danny took the wrong path.

Danny began his life in the United States in Santa Clara County, where he earned a handsome salary as an assembler for an electronics company and a computer component plant. In an effort to fulfill his obligations not only to his wife but to his parents, siblings, and in-laws who remained in Vietnam he worked overtime. He regularly sent them gifts of money and gold.

Danny still managed to save enough to take his first vacation. He decided to look up some old Chinese friends and enjoy a shopping spree. He flew to Hong Kong and was delighted to find his old friends. In one of the most expensive hotels in Kowloon, he discovered that his friends respected him—he was an American citizen now, and was obviously successful. Together they explored the nature of the sophisticated electronics market, discussing items that might readily be sold in Asia: computer parts, microchips, and other high-tech equipment. Danny and his business friends made some commitments and toasted one another.

Back at the electronics plant, Danny took particular interest in the stockrooms where the chips and other computer components were stored. At the same time, he began to visit cafés, nightclubs, and pool halls where he acquainted himself with the Vietnamese and Chinese-Vietnamese adolescents and young adults who hung around these spots. He befriended a few gang leaders. He knew that these people—their contacts and skills—would be useful.

He stole chips in small quantities—tiny and inexpensive chips, at first. He felt his way along and grew confident, delivering and selling the chips himself to buyers in San Francisco and Los Angeles. Gradually he built up his inventory.

Danny now entered a new phase. He cemented his connections and expanded his list of clients. He began to build relationships with employees of other electronics companies in Santa Clara County and continued to pilfer chips worth thousands of dollars from his own employer. Eventually he stopped making the deliveries himself. Teaming up with gang members from other cities in order to avoid identification, he hired juveniles—at two thousand dollars per trip—to transport the chips from the Silicon Valley to Los Angeles. He provided them with shotguns and pistols.

Danny bought himself a brand-new BMW. Not long afterward he bought a big house, equipped himself with a pager, and put a cellular phone in his BMW. His wife quit her job as a restaurant hostess and drove around town in a new Cadillac Seville.

He began to steal more expensive chips, which he sold locally at about one thousand dollars each. He packed the chips in ordinary-looking boxes and shipped them out to Los Angeles, Santa Ana, and San Diego via his teenage gang network. As he established connections with employees of other electronics manufacturers he increased his line of goods, and more and more money came in. His wife began to gamble. He bought her a fifty-thousand-dollar Mercedes Benz. She asked why he no longer brought the stuff home. "*Di dem co ngay gap ma*," Danny replied (One may run into ghosts if one keeps going out in the darkness of the night).

More cautious now, he stopped stealing from his own company. Besides, he had access to far more of the chips than he could market. He passed around price lists to gang members who hung out in pool halls in the seedier sections of San Jose, and made friends with powerful people in Santa Clara who laundered his money. Now his supply sources were not only in Santa Clara County, but in Stockton and Sacramento.

As his business increased in size and scope, Danny withdrew into the background. Two cronies handled his contacts and transactions, and for security reasons, he relied exclusively on Vietnamese gang members to deliver the goods. All sales were cash-and-carry. He immediately dismissed suspicious delivery boys.

The volume of his business grew to the point that Danny warehoused his inventories. He traveled to Hong Kong nearly every month to expand his market. This brought him the income he needed to invest in land and mutual funds. He added another BMW to the family fleet. His wife began to lose more and more money gambling.

His contacts in Hong Kong asked for more expensive items—disk chips and computer components valued at five hundred dollars or more each. New markets opened up in Singapore, Macao, and Hong Kong. Danny's business was international now. He bought exits from Vietnam for his parents, siblings, and in-laws under the United States Orderly Departure Program.

Growing uneasy, Danny wondered if perhaps it was time to get out of the computer chip business. He decided to diversify. He toyed with the notion of smuggling wristwatches, gold, and automobiles into Vietnam via Cambodia, but changed his mind. Instead, he chose to invest in local businesses and use front men. Increasingly, Danny felt nervous, even paranoid. No longer did he allow the rank and file to see his face. Those he suspected he had executed.

The money came in much faster than he could handle it, so he decided to do a little gambling himself: he and his wife tried their luck in Reno, Lake Tahoe, Las Vegas. One Saturday morning they flew to Las Vegas as part of MGM's "special guests" program; as usual, they planned to return to San Jose on Sunday. They never returned home. Local Big Brothers have told my wards that they have seen them on the streets of Hong Kong. Perhaps Danny and his wife had in mind the ancient wisdom *Di dem co ngay gap ma*—and chose to disappear.

A Serious Social Problem

The people in these stories have one thing in common: each was a criminal and became involved with gangs. . . . Unbeknownst to their parents, the three Nguyen brothers belonged to the notorious Oriental Boyz. And Danny's story illustrates the costly connection between white collar crime and gangs.

More than 800,000 Vietnamese live in the United States, and in some states their numbers have doubled in less than a decade. The vast majority of these people are law-abiding citizens and have established themselves in the community. . . .

But the fraction that is not—the fraction that has emerged as a criminal group—has become a serious social problem. In 1981 the FBI began to observe "emerging groups of criminals from outside of the United States," and its study included Asian criminal groups. In its analysis of Vietnamese criminal activity, completed for the Justice Department in March 1993, the FBI observed that the crime rate in the Vietnamese community was "grossly disproportionate" to its size and that "the people in these self-contained communities rated crime . . . as their priority problem."

This is because Vietnamese criminals most often commit crimes against other Vietnamese. The following account from the *San Jose Mercury News* is typical:

> Three armed Vietnamese robbers, one brandishing an Uzi-type weapon, forced their way into an East San Jose house where 18 Vietnamese were holding a family reunion and ransacked the home for two hours, terrorizing the occupants. The young robbers herded the occupants into a downstairs bedroom and tied [up] three men, kick-

ing some of them in the ribs. . . . The suspects are aware that affluent members of Vietnamese communities often keep large amounts of cash and other valuables in their homes and on their persons instead of in banks.

However, as the attack on the Good Guys electronics store and Danny's activities illustrate, the larger community is hardly immune to the predations of gangs. In California, . . . gang robbery and extortion alone cost private businesses and individuals millions of dollars annually, and rape, assault, and murder take a grisly human toll. . . .

Children from all ethnic groups join gangs, but according to federal investigators, Asian American criminal groups are growing faster than any other. Their illegal activities range from drug trafficking, money laundering, bribery, and extortion, to alien smuggling, home invasions, computer-technology theft, credit card counterfeiting, prostitution, gambling, and murder. And Asian American criminals are increasingly skilled in the way they commit crimes. In 1992, after twenty months of surveillance and information gathering by the Bureau of Alcohol, Tobacco and Firearms, the FBI, the Drug Enforcement [Administration], the Immigration and Naturalization Service, and the police departments of Santa Ana and Garden Grove, sixty Asian Americans were arrested on charges ranging from drug use and trafficking to homicide. The agencies involved in this operation agreed that the group was extraordinarily sophisticated in its methods.

The sophistication of Asian American gangs is also reflected in the fact that local gangs work hard to develop relationships with Asian American gangs elsewhere. They use these relationships to commit crimes at considerable distances from their home cities. Vietnamese gangs in particular are well organized and have achieved great degrees of mobility in their efforts to exploit new resources. Vietnamese gangs cooperate with one another to plan joint operations that, in some cases, are conducted thousands of miles away. A Santa Clara member of a Vietnamese gang, for example, flew to Boston to direct the robbery of a jewelry store and returned with over two hundred thousand dollars as his share of the loot. More typically, criminal operations are conducted within the state. Law enforcement officials note, however, that with increasing frequency juvenile criminals and their adult leaders are willing to fly to Houston, Dallas, New York, Florida, and even Hawaii to traffic in drugs and exploit vulnerable Vietnamese communities.

The FBI reports that as of spring 1993, Vietnamese criminal activity "can best be described as being in a state of accelerated networking, the precursor to organization." Vietnamese criminal activity is not—at least not yet—"organized crime." But senior research analysts for the New York City Criminal Justice Agency agree that the growth of Asian American gangs on the west coast is a microcosm of what is happening in major cities across the United States and around the world.

An Elderly Vietnamese American Adjusts to Life in America

Ba Tam, with James M. Freeman

Most Vietnamese immigrants living in America face tremendous changes. A particular challenge is adapting to new family structures. For example, the American nuclear family is a much smaller version of the more broadly inclusive Vietnamese family. The Vietnamese family often includes aunts, uncles, and grandparents, all living under one roof. Elderly Vietnamese Americans often have difficulty adjusting to unfamiliar social arrangements. Ba Tam, the author of this selection, feels sad that she cannot enjoy her last years in the way she would have been able to in Vietnam. She is unhappy living with her daughter's family, and feels neglected. Among the things she misses are the social interactions with her peers and the trips to Buddhist pagodas. Two years after this interview, in 1986, Ba Tam moved away from her daughter's family to live with other elderly Vietnamese. James M. Freeman, who wrote down her story, is a writer and editor.

I tried to get out of Vietnam since 1975. Because my daughter lived in America, I hoped to be able to leave, but the soldiers at the American Embassy refused to let me board the airplane. From that time on, my daughter tried to get me out. Because I am old, the Viet Cong did not make any difficulties for me. They give a hard time only to the young people and to big families.

My daughter says that she does not mind helping me with food, but she is afraid for my health. She cannot afford to pay for my health coverage, and I do not qualify for Medicare, since I am not a refugee, but an immigrant who came to America under the Orderly Departure Program.

I was happy! America! It is just like heaven! Because people live here in *freedom*. You can go anywhere. You can live richer. Over here I see people go by in cars, but in Vietnam people ride bicycles and are poor.

I remember that when I first came here, I could not recognize my daughter, whom I had not seen since 1962, but she recognized me, even though I was old and very skinny. Because of the difference in hours, it took me about a week to adjust to night and day in America.

I also got used to American food; I can eat American food! My daughter cooks American food, and she and her Vietnamese husband live and eat like Americans: salad, canned food, barbecued chicken, no soup.

I Am Sad

I'm sad, though, because my daughter's children speak only English. Also, at my daughter's house, I do nothing. My daughter won't let me do anything because she thinks everything is strange for me. She tells me to rest. But I cannot stay doing nothing. My daughter does not let me cook; she does the cooking, and I water the garden. I help them clean house after eating. On Saturday my daughter turns to the Vietnamese broadcast because she thinks that I am sad. I regret I don't know how to speak English. I can speak French, and I *will* learn how to speak English.

In Vietnam, every family, even Christians, must have an altar to worship ancestors, and the Buddha too. But not here in America. I never see any houses with altars here.

My religion is Buddhism. I went to pagodas all the time.

In Vietnam, we have monks who preach Buddhist religion on Sundays and formal days, and I went to the pagoda at those times. I've not yet visited a pagoda in America.

I notice that Vietnamese people in America don't go to the pagoda a lot because they live far away. They rarely have free time. I miss not going to the pagoda because I have just arrived here. In Vietnam I used the bus to visit friends and the pagoda. It's cheaper. Over here, my children must go to work. They don't have time to drive me. This is my major concern; I am *very sad*. In Vietnam, we went by pedicab or Lambretta, the three-wheel cycle, which could carry several people. We moved around a lot, either with these vehicles or by walking. Over here in America, I can walk only a couple of kilometers; then I get tired.

In Vietnam, under the Communists, people like me who were over the working age of 60 could wander freely all about the town. Nobody bothered us; no one created trouble as long as we didn't involve ourselves in politics. It was easy for us to travel. I went all over, sometimes to coffee shops, sometimes to big restaurants. At first these were reserved only for the Viet Cong, but later they let in everyone. The prices were cheap. My friends and I would buy beer, cola, orange, and sweet cakes, sometimes even ice cream.

In Vietnam, in a village, from one end to another, everybody knows each other. Even in the city where I lived, we knew each other and visited one another. If I was sick, my friends visited me, and I did the same for them. I would see my friends at the market. When I think of that, I miss not having people I know nearby. It's very sad. Over here I live at home, and I cannot go anywhere. In Vietnam, if I felt sad, I'd go to visit my friends, my fellow "sisters."

Older Vietnamese people who come to America write letters back home. They don't have work or jobs to do, even though they are active people, so it is sad for them.

Because there are lots of cars here, they do not walk. My daughter warns me that I may be run over by cars, so I am afraid to walk. In Vietnam, we went to the pagoda or to friends; here we stay at home. I want to find something to do, but cannot find anything suitable. I am very sad, and I have nowhere to go.

Vietnamese Americans Today Face Many Challenges

Max Niedzwiecki and Doua Thor

In 2005 Max Niedzwiecki and Doua Thor gave testimony, from which this selection was taken, before the President's Advisory Commission on Asian Americans and Pacific Islanders. In it they outline the major opportunities and challenges facing Vietnamese Americans today. They discuss the high poverty and disability rates among Southeast Asians and call on the government to provide more assistance to these Americans. Niedzwiecki and Doua are members of the Southeast Asia Resource Action Center (SEARAC), an organization dedicated to promoting the rights of immigrants and refugees from Southeast Asia.

Max Niedzwiecki is executive director of the Southeast Asia Resource Action Center. Doua Thor is the organization's deputy director.

As a former refugee and now an American citizen, I am honored to have the opportunity to speak to the [President's Advisory Commission on Asian Americans and Pacific Islanders] today [January 24, 2005] regarding the challenges as well as successes of the Southeast Asian community in America. I was born in Laos, escaped to Thailand, lived in Ban Vinai refugee camp, and came to the United States with my own family fleeing persecution be-

Max Niedzwiecki and Doua Thor, "Opportunities and Challenges for Economic Development Among Americans from Cambodia, Laos, and Vietnam: Education, Disability, and Community Organizations," President's Advisory Commission on Asian Americans and Pacific Islanders, White House Initiative on Asian Americans and Pacific Islanders, Washington, DC, January 24, 2005.

cause my father was a Hmong soldier fighting for the United States. For refugees and communities from the countries of Cambodia, Laos, and Vietnam, economic and community development must be carried out through a holistic approach. For our communities, economic and community development are closely connected to opportunities for education, support for "mutual assistance associations" (community based organizations created by and led mostly by former refugees using their own experience to serve the community), and programs targeting multiple barriers such as language that Southeast Asian families in poverty face on a daily basis.

My name is Doua Thor and I currently serve as the Deputy Director of the Southeast Asia Resource Action Center, also known as SEARAC. Based in Washington, DC, SEARAC is a national nonprofit refugee organization managed primarily by and for Americans with heritage in Cambodia, Laos, and Vietnam. SEARAC advances the interest of the Southeast Asian community through leadership development, capacity building, public policy advocacy, and community empowerment. Dr. Max Niedzwiecki, SEARAC's Executive Director, and I will provide this testimony jointly.

Most "Southeast Asian Americans" from Cambodia, Laos, and Vietnam are refugees who have resettled in the U.S. since 1975, or they are the children of refugees. Contrary to the model minority myth, the majority of Southeast Asian Americans continue to struggle with economic, educational, and other challenges to a degree seldom understood by policy makers and government institutions. Many of the challenges facing the communities remain unaddressed: for example, the strong link between poverty and high disability rates in some groups has been largely ignored up to this point. Southeast Asian Americans are *not* the "model minority [meaning unusually successful immigrants]," and they require increased attention from policy makers. In addressing community needs, policy makers can partner with a network of over 180 . . . community-based and faith-based organizations that are managed primarily by and for Southeast Asian Americans.

A Brief History

Refugees from Cambodia, Laos, and Vietnam began arriving in the United States in large numbers after the Vietnam War in 1975. They resettled in America because they had no other choice: by definition refugees are fleeing "a well-founded fear of persecution." 2005 marks the 30th anniversary of their communities' establishment in the U.S., and they now number approximately two million nationwide, with populations of over 40,000 in California, Florida, Georgia, Massachusetts, Minnesota, Pennsylvania, Texas, Virginia, the State of Washington, and Wisconsin. They are extremely diverse in terms of language and culture. Main cultural and language groups include Vietnamese, Cambodian (or Khmer), Hmong (or Mong), and Lao. Other groups include Iu Mien (or Mien), Khmu, Montagnard, Taidam, and ethnic Chinese. Vietnamese Americans alone number over 1.2 million.

Although refugee flows from Southeast Asia have decreased significantly since the 1980s, approximately 15,000 Hmong refugees originally from Laos are expected to enter the U.S. during fiscal years 2004 and 2005, and hundreds or thousands of Montagnard and ethnic Vietnamese refugees from Vietnam are likely to enter this year [2005] as well. In addition, well over half a million non-refugee immigrants have entered the U.S. from Cambodia, Laos, and Vietnam since the 1950s.

Education, Poverty, and Disability

Because most Southeast Asian Americans are from refugee backgrounds, many of them face challenges that are less common among other Asian American groups, as well as among Caucasian Americans. Here we will touch on only three areas of concern: education, poverty, and disability.

Many refugees, and especially those from Cambodia and Laos, arrived in the U.S. from rural, farming backgrounds, without having had access to formal education. Even today, Southeast Asian Americans are less likely than others to have reached high levels of education. For example, according to the 2000 Census, over 56 percent of Hmong women aged 25 and over had had "no formal schooling" whatsoever, as did over 31 percent of Cambodian women, over 27 percent of Laotian women, and over 9 percent of Vietnamese women—compared with only 1.3 percent for American women considered overall. Likewise, college graduation rates in the communities tend to be low. Just over 9 percent of Cambodian adults were found to have a bachelors degree or higher, as were just over 7 percent of Hmong, over 7 percent of Laotians, and over 20 percent of Vietnamese—compared with nearly 25 percent of Americans considered overall. These college graduation rates for Southeast Asian Americans show drastic improvement since the 1990 Census, and the communities have many "success stories," but much progress must still be made. Although the U.S. offers educational opportunities that were absent in much of Southeast Asia, it is still difficult for parents without much formal education to mentor their children when it comes to school; and for a variety of reasons it is still more difficult for low-income people to succeed academically, whatever their race or immigration history might be.

Education and poverty are interconnected among Southeast Asian Americans, as they are among other groups. Many Southeast Asian American communities demonstrate strikingly high poverty rates. The 2000 Census found that in 1999 the per capita income for Americans considered overall was $21,587. Cambodians were found to have per capita incomes of $10,215, Hmong of $6,613, Laotians of $11,454, and Vietnamese of $15,385. In fact, Hmong were found to have the lowest per capita income of any ethnic group described by the 2000 Census, the second lowest being Tohono O'Odham Native Americans with $8,395. Poverty rates were also found to be high among Southeast Asian Americans: over 29 percent of Cambodians, 37 percent of Hmong, 19 percent of Laotians, and 16 percent of Vietnamese were found to be living in poverty in 1999, compared with just over 12 percent of Americans overall.

Many factors contribute to enduring poverty among Southeast Asian Americans. Education is certainly an important factor, as are the fact that many refugees arrive in the U.S. without marketable job skills, the fact that many arrive in this country without knowledge of English or native-language literacy, and the fact that under current law elderly and disabled refugees who have not obtained citizenship are limited to seven years of Supplemental Security Income (SSI) in most states. Rev. Y Hin Nie, the Pastor of the United Montagnard Christian Church in Greensboro, NC, often tells us about members of his church who arrived in the U.S. alone at an advanced age and have lost their SSI benefits. They find it very difficult to learn English, and have not been able to pass citizenship tests or find jobs in North Carolina's challenging economy. They rely upon charity from the church in order to survive, and given the economic limitations of church members this creates an unfair burden for the entire community. This kind of hardship is playing out in many states.

These factors, and others, require further attention from policymakers, although efforts have begun to address them. One factor contributing to poverty in the communities, which has received little attention up to this point, is disability. In all American communities, disabled people are more likely to live in poverty. According to the 2000 Census, Southeast Asian Americans are more likely to be disabled than are Americans considered overall, and disability and poverty are more closely related.

According to the 2000 Census, approximately 19 percent of Americans considered overall, and 17 percent of Asian Americans overall, report having at least one disability. Southeast Asian Americans are more likely to be disabled: Approximately 24 percent of Cambodians, 21 percent of Hmong, 22 percent of Laotians, and 22 percent of Vietnamese report at least one disability. . . .

In many communities the U.S. Census indicates that almost half of the householders of the lowest-income households are disabled.

Despite barriers such as widespread disability, Southeast Asian Americans have continued to be innovative in promoting the economic well-being of their families and the community as a whole. Much of this innovation is centered at community-based organizations.

Mutual Assistance Associations

Southeast Asian Americans have created many hundreds of formal and informal organizations and associations for community self-help. Often the secular organizations are referred to as "mutual assistance associations" or MAAs, and the religious ones such as temples and churches as "faith-based organizations" or FBOs. The Southeast Asia Resource Action Center (SEARAC) works with a national network of over 180 MAAs and FBOs that are grant-eligible and have combined annual budgets well over $75 million. The Director of the U.S. Office of Refugee Resettlement (ORR), Dr. Nguyen Van Hanh, has correctly referred to these community-rooted organizations as one of the "three pillars of the Refugee Program," along with partners in state government, and voluntary resettlement agencies or "volags." SEARAC is proud to support MAAs and FBOs through many projects, including the first federally-funded project to increase the service capacities of refugee FBOs and CBOs (community-based organizations such as MAAs): the Values, Empowerment, Resources and Betterment project, or VERB, which is funded through the Department of Health and Human Service's Compassion Capital Fund.

Of the 182 organizations in SEARAC's network, 84 offer economic empowerment programs in areas such as job training, microenterprise development, and individual development accounts or IDAs. An additional 54 offer assistance to their clients in accessing social service benefits. Other common program areas include interpretation and translation, youth services, cultural preservation, community celebrations, advocacy, services to elders, citizenship training, and health education. These organizations offer services that are cultural and linguistically appropriate, and that annually help thousands of families become economically self-sufficient. In many communities, they serve as essential bridges between communities that are still adjusting to life in the U.S., and the communities and institutions that surround them. . . .

Strategies for Empowerment

Our recommendations to the President's Advisory Commission on Asian Americans and Pacific Islanders are the following:

1. Remember when making public statements about Asian Americans and Pacific Islanders that some communities continue to struggle economically, educationally, and in other ways. They are *not* the "model minority," and to describe them in those terms decreases the chances that their actual needs and strengths will be taken seriously by decision-

makers in government and other sectors.

2. Remind your colleagues that in order to effectively promote economic development among Southeast Asian Americans, policymakers must also promote educational achievement, services and programs that support disabled people and their families, and other initiatives that impact upon well-being. Economic empowerment can best be fostered through approaches that attack the root causes of poverty.

3. Support efforts to strengthen Southeast Asian American community-based and faith-based organizations through increased funding, training, and technical assistance. These organizations are essential partners to hundreds of public agencies across the nation, as well as direct providers of uniquely effective services that foster self-sufficiency.

CHAPTER 4

Accomplished Vietnamese Americans

COMING TO AMERICA

Le Ly Hayslip: Author

John Lee

Le Ly Hayslip is the author of two autobiographies: *When Heaven and Earth Changed Places* and *Child of War, Woman of Peace*. The two memoirs formed the basis of the movie *Heaven and Earth*, directed by Oliver Stone. In her teenage years Le Ly Hayslip delivered messages and set booby traps for the pro-Communist Viet Cong fighters. For these activities she was beaten and tortured by South Vietnamese officers. Then the Viet Cong began to suspect that she was a spy. Facing persecution from both sides, Hayslip moved from her home village of Ky La to Saigon and eventually escaped from Vietnam in 1970.

In this 1994 article journalist John Lee describes Hayslip's work on her memoirs and her interaction with Stone while making her books into a movie. Lee also explains how she established the East Meets West Foundation, an organization dedicated to philanthropic endeavors in both the United States and Vietnam.

In the Vietnam of Le Ly Hayslip's childhood, the land told secrets to those who would just listen. There were whispers of inevitable suffering, and also of coping—if only to suffer again. The secrets revealed much about life: it was a lush, verdant existence, one that had a tendency to all too suddenly turn to dirt.

Hayslip learned well the whispers of the Vietnamese landscape, and decades later committed two autobiographical works to print, chronicling her experiences as a peasant girl, Viet Cong guerilla, prisoner of war, G.I. prosti-

John Lee, "A Woman of the Land: *A. Magazine*'s John Lee Speaks with Le Ly Hayslip, Author and Survivor," *A. Magazine*, December 1, 1994, p. 37. Copyright © 1994 by Le Ly Hayslip. Reproduced by permission.

tute, single mother, war refugee, and self-styled "American businesswoman." She translated the land's language into the literary stuff of world-class storytellers, and, by writing for an English-speaking audience, came to capture the imagination of filmmaker Oliver Stone.

The narrative of Hayslip's lives inspired the first screenplay Stone has written and directed with a female protagonist—one small indication of the extraordinary existence Hayslip led in Vietnam, and has continued since immigrating to the United States in 1970. Readers of *When Heaven and Earth Changed Places*, Hayslip's first book, co-written with Jay Wurts, and *Child of War, Woman of Peace*, written with her oldest son, Jimmy, learn not only of the eventfulness of her life, but of the profound connection between the spirit of a people, and the earth from which they derive nourishment. Although written in simple prose, her story is a subtle and lyrical telling—not the easiest material for cinematic adaptation. Especially by Hollywood, at the hands of a director infamous as a headstrong maverick.

Creating Art from Pain

To appreciate the unlikely position Hayslip was in when Hollywood came knocking, it helps to picture an immigrant woman who came to the United States at the age of 20, having just wed an American army contractor 35 years her senior. She has been three times a mother, twice widowed, and survived her first husband's death by emphysema, her second by apparent suicide. After 14 years of rearing her sons in the suburbs of San Diego, she realized that she had volumes of stories to relate within her, but not a lick of writing or publishing know-how. She knew only that she had felt much hardship, and as she has related to friends, believed she was on the receiving end of a punishing karmic cycle; her role was to somehow use her bad experiences to create good. "My life story is that of an individual raised in a small village, and forced to live between victims . . . on two sides," Hayslip says today. "I fought for my country against America. Later, I became American, and my sons are American. I am on both sides, and I love both sides. . . . My biggest question is: How do we live on this earth together?"

She wrote her memories longhand on a stack of yellow legal pads, then had her son Jimmy enter the material into a computer. She sent the manuscript to coauthor Wurts, who fine-tuned her writing, then sent her files back for second and third revisions. After two years of reviving and writing memories, she returned to Vietnam for the first time in more than a decade and a half. She visited relatives who were suffering from the postwar legacy in and around her native village, Ky La. She saw streets serving as home to legions of children—orphans of war and poverty. The area's lone hospital was more primitive than the one there when she emigrated in the '70s.

With her new knowledge of Vietnam's suffering as an inspiration, she returned to the states, sold her successful restaurant business, and established the East Meets West Foundation, a nonprofit organization that arranges medical and educational aid between the United States and Vietnam. The foundation often took her to the Bay Area, away from her sons, but where there was more support for her efforts. The foundation work gave urgency to her writing—a book would be the best way to reach Americans and explain the plight of her native country. "I was born to be a perfect wife," she says. "Marry the boy next door. Make my father proud. Worship our ancestors. Take care of my water buffalo. But look, bombs are dropping down, killing people left and right. How can I just be a perfect farm girl?"

In 1989, after five long years of writing had passed, *When Heaven and Earth Changed Places* was hailed in the *New York Times Book Review* as "a testimony to the intelligence, unflinching honesty, and simple clarity of Le Ly Hayslip's voice." Hayslip's literary agent had already begun fielding calls from filmmakers seeking the rights to her story.

She considered an offer by actress Joan Chen, who had read an unpublished manuscript of *When Heaven and Earth Changed Places* and expressed deep affinity for Hayslip's saga. Chen's standing as perhaps the only Asian woman in Hollywood with the notoriety to attract studio backing for such a project led to negotiations, and the actress secured a commitment from Ron Bass, the screenwriter who went on to cowrite the film adaptation of the first Asian American blockbuster, *The Joy Luck Club*. With a certifiable Asian American female star pledging to do the *Heaven and Earth* story as a labor of love, why did Hayslip go with Stone—a Caucasian, and a man?

Hayslip had been warned that Stone's track record for eliciting sensitive female portrayals left much to be desired. Women appeared in Stone productions only as human props for raging flights of male fancy. Asian characters, particularly Vietnamese, fared even worse, Hayslip was told. "Lots of people say he did some bad things," Hayslip says. "When we met, I had seen the movie about [Jim Morrison], and I couldn't help but say 'I hope you don't want to make this a film like *The Doors*.' He just laughed and said, 'Oh, it's totally different.'"

"We talked about my book, and about my village, and philosophy, and Vietnam. He had an energy that made him seem open and honest. After the talk, I had confidence. It was mostly intuition, but I had the feeling he was a good man."

According to Hayslip, Joan Chen had deferred her claim by the time Stone negotiated film rights to the book. All parties agreed that having Stone's name attached would not only bring industry attention and financial wherewithal to the film, it would also benefit Hayslip's U.S.-Vietnam aid projects. And, in her heart, that is what this Hollywood turn was about. Stone agreed to give Hayslip unprecedented license to review the screenplay (which lifts liberally from the books) and to serve as consultant on location. She has also conducted more than 300 interviews to promote the film and the foundation, and has been to premieres in Los Angeles, New York, and Japan, Australia and seven European countries since last December [1993].

When promotional touring for the film finally ends, Hayslip says that she would like to resettle. She lives now in a small apartment in San Francisco, and is unhappy about the distance separating her from her mother in Ky La, and children in Southern California. Since 1984, Hayslip's family and personal lives have been put on hold. At 44, she is ready for yet another change. "For the last five years, whatever was in my personal life went on the side. I have an 86-year-old mother and an 18-year-old son. . . . More and more I'm thinking, my younger son is not with me, my mother's not with me, what am I doing in this world?"

Of the places Hayslip has been in the United States, she likes North County San Diego best, having lived there for seven years before moving to San Francisco last fall [1993]. She often finds herself thinking about her house in Escondido, just off Via Rancho Parkway, where the highway from San Diego dissolves into two-laners. There, in the countryside, pasture land trades licks with furrowed fields and low hills; if you half-close your eyes, you might imagine you are back in Vietnam. Hayslip says she likes the quiet there. It gives her a chance to meditate on what a woman like her is supposed to do next.

A chance to listen to the land.

Tony Bui: Film Director

Tony Bui, interviewed by Rob Blackwelder

After arriving in the United States at the age of two, moviemaker Tony Bui and the rest of his family eventually settled in Sunnyvale, California. His father operated a video store, and eventually Bui showed an interest in making his own movies. He attended film school at Loyola Marymount University, and made numerous trips to Vietnam as part of his research for his first two films, *Yellow Lotus* and *Three Seasons*. In 1999 *Three Seasons* became the first film shot in Vietnam by an American director.

In this 1999 interview Bui tells journalist Rob Blackwelder about his philosophy of making movies. Bui wants to make movies that have meaning, and he especially hopes to give voice to the Vietnamese people he has grown to love.

Tony Bui is 100 percent Californian. The 26-year-old darling of the 1999 Sundance Film Festival has long, ponytailed hair, a casual demeanor and laid-back, West Coast accent—which might just as easily be peppered with "whoa, dudes" as insights on filmmaking. All of this is evidence of his Americanized upbringing by Vietnamese parents who fled their homeland with 2-year-old Tony and his older brother in 1975.

Yet the young writer-director—whose interest in filmmaking was sparked by thousands of free rentals from his father's video store as a teenager—chose the hardships of life in the country of his birth as the topic of his first feature film, even though he'd never even visited Vietnam until a very few years ago.

"I wanted to bring to the screen what I saw there," Bui explained when we met in March [1999] to talk about his movie, "and to give voice to the people that I met and became friends with and care about."

Yellow Lotus, his award-winning short from three years ago, garnered him an invitation to the hallowed workshops of the Sundance Filmmaker's Institute in 1997, where he put the finishing touches on a script for the magical but matter-of-fact allegory on modern Vietnam called *Three Seasons*. In January [1999], Bui and his picture—which has just been missed in major markets—cleaned up at Sundance, taking home the Grand Jury prize for best picture, another nod for best cinematography, and the box office-friendly Audience Award.

Movie Milestones

Aided by the influence of two high-profile project cheerleaders—cast members Harvey Keitel in the States and Don Duong (a respected Vietnamese actor who happens to be Bui's uncle) in Saigon [Ho Chi Minh City now]—Bui's film became the first American production allowed to shoot in his native country since the war, and the first American film made entirely in Vietnamese.

Three Seasons tells a trio of parallel stories about the rapidly changing face of this formerly closed society. One follows an impoverished cyclo driver, another a homeless boy and the third a lotus harvester, and each takes place in Saigon during a different season (dry, wet and growth). The film is so rich with the flavor of this captivating but underdeveloped city, and so refreshingly devoid of war references and Western perspective, that when Bui was in San Francisco for the city's film festival premiere of *Three Seasons*, I had to ask him how he gained his seemingly native perspective and how he got in touch with the difficult day-to-day existence of the Vietnamese lower caste when he had grown up so detached from his roots.

Rob Blackwelder: When did you first start going back to Vietnam? Did you go back as a tourist? Did you go back to see family?

Tony Bui: I went back to see family. My mom sent me back. I was 19 and I'd never really even left this country, except to maybe go to Tijuana or something. I was sent to Vietnam basically to visit my grandparents, who were ailing, and I hated it. I hated every moment of it. I remember arriving there, I remember the cabin doors opening and the humidity hitting me, and the dust, and all the noise, and the smells, and the crowds, and the rickshaws, everything around me. The city has changed so much since then, and now I'm glad I was there for what was a transitional period. But I remember the first four hours I was there I just wanted to go back home.

You wanted to get right back on the plane.

That's what I wanted to do, absolutely. And I was there for two weeks. Then, I remember, I found one restaurant, in District One, that actually had air conditioning, and I planned all my day's events around that restaurant. I literally went in there four or five times a day—"Uh, I just want a Coke." (Laughs).

And after two weeks, I left, never thinking I would go back. I landed in San Francisco and in about a 45 minute drive to my parents' house in San Jose, I just had this incredible feeling of depression that hit me. It was very odd because I wanted so badly to leave and (here) I had this incredible sense of longing and sadness. I was in tears. But I couldn't explain what I was crying about. I had to go back to figure it out. And I remember writing apology letters to all my relatives, because I'm sure I insulted them every day with "What do you mean you don't have a toilet?" and "Oh my god, it's so hot!" and "What's that smell?!?"

So the next term break I had, I went back and spent three and a half months there, and this time I really experienced it the way I should have the first time. I embraced all the things I had hated about it, and to this day I love the heat, I love all the smells, I love all the nuances. And now it's all those nuances that call me back.

And you were going back as a tourist at this point, not as a filmmaker?

As a total civilian, absolutely. I was a student, so all I had at one time was maybe a hundred bucks, you know. At that time, a hundred bucks could sort of last you a few months, but I never ate in the restaurants, I never stayed at the hotels, so my entire experience in Vietnam was on a very, very local level. That's how I got to know all the cyclo drivers, and got to know all the street kids, and got to know many of the people I wrote about and cared about. It didn't come from any desire to make a film about it. I didn't think it was even possible.

But at that point you were headed down the film career road, were you not?

Yes. I was just going into film school.

But it was two separate things?

Two separate things happening. They would meet very quickly, but it was two separate things. (So) I was seeing this Vietnam that I had never thought about or seen or heard about growing up—because everything I'd heard was always about the past.

Was there a lot of discussion about Vietnam in your house?

There was, but even that was about the past. My dad was in the military, and obviously we escaped. So a lot of his stories were about the past, about the hardships, about the cruelty of the communists. But when I went there, I experienced a totally different world. I saw this incredible spirit, this incredible humanity that was very universal and had nothing to do with what I thought about Vietnam growing up. Soon I was then going back every year. Sometimes twice a year. Then at the same time this was happening, I was immersed in film school. I began to identify with films that were personal for the filmmakers, films that had a consciousness, films that try to say something, films that meant something. And film school in 1995 was very much the [filmmaker Quentin] Tarantino age, the slacker age. But while I was watching those films and having a good time, those weren't the films that were affecting me.

So these two things are happening separately (but) by 1994 the two came together, and I realized at that point the kind of filmmaker I wanted to be—a filmmaker that could hopefully say something, hopefully reveal something. I wanted to make personal films, films that I could care about.

Dat Nguyen:
Professional Athlete

Adam Piore

Dat Nguyen, the first Vietnamese American professional football player, has helped break down racial barriers and change attitudes in the racially divided town of his youth. In this 2001 profile, journalist Adam Piore explores Dat Nguyen's childhood in Rockport, Texas, a town bitterly divided during the influx of Vietnamese refugee fishermen in the 1970s. After Dat Nguyen's successful football career at Texas A&M University, the Dallas Cowboys recruited him as a middle linebacker.

Adam Piore is a former reporter for *Cambodia Daily*. He covered events in Cambodia, Vietnam, and Indonesia for many western papers. Piore also trained journalists in Phnom Penh, Cambodia, before becoming a correspondent for *Newsweek*.

If any other group of kids had won the Rockport-Fulton youth soccer championship in Texas, the parents of their opponents would surely have applauded. But most of the members of Dat Nguyen's team were the children of Vietnamese refugees. So when the proud victors rose to accept their trophies, the crowd showered them with boos. It was the 1980s, and back then tensions were so high in the small south Texas coastal community that white shrimpers and their Vietnamese competitors sometimes carried rifles into the bay and took potshots at one another from their boats.

Dat Nguyen's domination on the soccer field (he scored as many as 10 goals a game) didn't make his team any more popular with the locals. "We weren't wanted in that community," Nguyen recalled. "They wanted to kick us out. There was so much hatred between the two cultures. My parents told me we couldn't trust anybody outside our family."

Firsts in Football

Nobody in Rockport would dare boo Dat Nguyen now. The hard-headed kid who brawled on the field to defend himself against racist taunts grew up to become the closest thing Texans have to royalty. Nguyen became a 5-foot, 11-inch, 231-pound football star. After leading Rockport-Fulton High School to statewide renown, Nguyen went on to play at Texas A&M where he broke the school record for tackles and in 1998 was named the best defensive player in the country. Last week [January 2001] Nguyen, now 25, finished his second season as a middle linebacker for "America's Team," the Dallas Cowboys. The easygoing, quick-to-smile athlete has broken a lot of barriers. He is the first Vietnamese-American ever to play pro football. He was the first Vietnamese-American to start at linebacker for a major university in Texas.

Breaking Racial Barriers

But equally remarkable are the barriers Nguyen has broken down in this tiny, racially divided corner of the United States. Thousands of Vietnamese refugees moved to the gulf coast of Texas in the 1970s, many drawn by the opportunity to make a living doing what they once did in Vietnam: shrimping. According to the U.S. Census, 1,112 Asian-Americans, the vast majority Vietnamese, live among a population of 23,129 in Nguyen's home county. At last count well over 70,000 Vietnamese lived in Texas. Dat Nguyen is the first to have a day named after him in his hometown, and the first to have his picture plastered on a billboard displayed on the way into city limits. "That boy never backed down for nobody," recalls Jimmy Hattenbach, Nguyen's old soccer coach and mentor. "He has helped to mend this community—everybody in this town believes that. When the football team started winning, it really brought the town together. He became a role model."

Nobody would have believed that was possible just a few years ago. Dat Nguyen's family fled Ben Da, a fishing village on South Vietnam's Vung Tau Peninsula, in a fishing boat, the night shells began to rain down on their village in April, 1975. Ho Nguyen, Dat's brother, remembers soldiers firing artillery at their boat from the shore. After brief stops at an Arkansas refugee camp, where Nguyen was born, and in Michigan, the family landed in another war zone. Thousands of Vietnamese shrimpers had already begun new lives in the bays of south Texas. When they began pulling around-the-clock shifts, the locals felt their livelihoods were threatened.

Soon things turned violent. Little more than 20 miles from the Rockport area, in the town of Seadrift, a Vietnamese shrimper shot and killed a local who was beating him up. Up and down the coast angry shrimpers burned boats, and the story received national attention. Tensions were not as high in Nguyen's hometown, a seaside community of rickety piers, Texas scrub brush, old houses and trailer-park vacation homes. But they were there. Leslie Casterline, owner of the Casterline Fish Co., used to buy shrimp from Ho Nguyen, Dat's father. He remembers the Vietnamese boats pulling up to the dock, and white shrimping boats pulling away in protest. Then one morning when Casterline arrived at work, a card fell off the door. "Youv've been paid a friendly visit by the Knights of the Ku Klux Klan. The next one might not be so friendly," he says it read. "People would come by and cuss us out.

But we just didn't have anything against the Vietnamese," Casterline said.

Changing Attitudes

Nguyen broke down the barriers on the sports field. In eighth grade, he began to play football. Just as he had on the soccer field, he always seemed to know where the ball was. He was exceptionally quick, and soon learned to tackle hard. In an area where two thirds of the population have been known to caravan to championship high-school games, people took notice. Attitudes began to change. "He was a celebrity in high school," said Trish Wilson, who worked in the school district's central office for 18 years. "He was just one of those kids you don't see too often. If he was out there on the field, he was going to do something. He'd always get the extra yards, make the tackle, save the day." In college, he was one of the most popular Aggies ever. And when the Dallas Cowboys drafted him in 1999, he became a fan favorite. Critics who always said he was too small, and that an Asian would never make it (only four people of Asian ancestry had done so) had been proved wrong.

Now the town that once booed Dat Nguyen has claimed him as their own. Last year [2000], Rockport held a Dat Nguyen Day to honor him. Three hundred people showed up. (When a campaigning governor named George W. Bush came to town a few years earlier, only 200 people turned out.) At the local Wal-Mart, store managers have created a consumer shrine to the football star, with Dat Nguyen T shirts hanging off a rack and hats bearing his name. This year his neighbors chipped in $15,000 to erect the billboard on the road into town.

Some in the area still cling to racist attitudes. Nguyen says he receives an occasional piece of hate mail. Interracial dating can lead to fistfights in waterfront bars. And some residents actively opposed erecting the celebratory billboard. But they are in the minority. When Nguyen returns to his hometown he is mobbed for autographs. "There's always going to be people who are going to have some tension against us," Nguyen says. "But I think the tension died down. I opened a lot of doors for people to see that whatever background you come from, everybody can have an opportunity. I dreamed of being here all my life. And now I'm a Vietnamese boy living in America, playing the American sport, living the American dream, playing for America's Team. It doesn't get any better than that."

Kieu Chinh: Actress

Emmanuelle Leal

Journalist Emmanuelle Leal reports in this selection that after Saigon fell to the Communist North Vietnamese, Vietnamese actress Kieu Chinh escaped to Canada. With help from actress Tippi Hedren, she was able to move to Hollywood, where she landed a recurring role on the hit TV series *M.A.S.H.* Later, she went on to act in many movies, including Amy Tan's *The Joy Luck Club.* Leal also reports that Kieu Chinh is the founder of the Vietnamese Children's Fund, an organization dedicated to building schools and spreading goodwill. Emmanuelle Leal is an assistant editor for the *Coyote Press*, a newspaper of the Community College of Southern Nevada (CCSN).

Movie star and humanitarian Kieu Chinh recently brought her story of survival and one woman's search for empowerment to CCSN students.

Kieu is best known for her role in the movie, *The Joy Luck Club.* As Suyuan, she portrayed a Chinese immigrant living in San Francisco struggling to teach traditional lessons to her American-born daughter.

Kieu told students at the Cheyenne campus of her struggle to overcome the sorrow and despair of war in her native Vietnam. She lost most of her family to the conflict that lasted from the 1940s to 1975, but nonetheless grew up to become the biggest female film star in Indochina.

But her fortunes would forever mirror those of her nation: changeable. From the height of stardom, Kieu even-

Emmanuelle Leal, "Actress Kieu Chinh Visits Cheyenne Campus, Brings Story of Struggle and Triumph from Vietnam to U.S.," www.coyotepressonline.com, February 1, 2001. Copyright © 2001 by *Coyote Press*. Reproduced by permission.

tually lost everything with the fall of Saigon in 1975. She would regain it all, albeit in another land and culture, the United States, by winning featured roles in the hit TV show, *M.A.S.H.*

"Orphaned" by War

Kieu grew up in Hanoi, Vietnam, during the French Indochina War from 1946 to 1954. Losing her mother at a young age, Kieu endured more hardships of war, at one time watching her home burned to the ground and being separated from her family. She basically became an orphan left to survive. During the time the French battled rebels in northern Vietnam, Kieu was sent by her father to southern Vietnam to escape the war.

Alone, and with her family still in northern Vietnam, Kieu faced a harsh reality: she was traumatized, alone, and fearful in unfamiliar South Vietnam. Adopted by a local family, Kieu became their maid and made them her new family and her new home. She was eventually married to her adopted family's eldest son and gave birth to a girl while her new husband moved to the U.S. to train as a paratrooper.

As Kieu walked past a movie director who happened to be looking for a Vietnamese woman who spoke English and French for a role in his movie, she caught his eye. After turning down the offer at the demand of her mother-in-law, Kieu later accepted another role as a Buddhist nun. Thus Kieu began her triumphant acting career in Asia.

Discovering a love for the art of acting, Kieu went on to produce a talk show which later became a hit. Eventually, she was signed on a contract to produce three movies—a move that made her the highest-paid Vietnamese actress. Just as her fame and new life began to take hold, Kieu lost everything during the fall of Saigon.

When Saigon fell to the North Vietnamese in 1975,

Kieu was forced to relinquish her passport. All her assets were frozen. Wanting to see her now three children, she arranged to be smuggled out of Vietnam by a friend. Kieu got as far as Singapore, where she was arrested for possessing a passport of a country that no longer existed.

Celebrity Brings Assistance

Kieu spent one day in jail, and was not allowed to make a phone call until she noticed her cell guard was reading a magazine with her picture on the cover. Pointing her own picture out to the guard, Kieu was allowed to make one phone call. Close friends paid for her release, and because she was a stateless person, Kieu could not stay in any one country for long. Traveling from country to country, Kieu grew tired and longed to hold her children in her arms.

Finally, after traveling throughout the world, Kieu arrived in Canada to be reunited with her children. She was relieved, but that feeling was replaced by heartbreak with the news that Saigon had fallen.

"My country, my home, had now belonged to another world," said Kieu. Becoming a Vietnamese refugee in Canada, Kieu had been left with nothing. Kieu needed a job, so she decided to call on her friends whom she had worked with in past movies.

She called Tippi Hedren, Melanie Griffith's mother, who sent her a plane ticket to Hollywood and helped Kieu get back on her feet. While staying with Hedren, Kieu met many celebrities and went with Tippi to the movie premiere of *Jaws*. At the premiere, she caught the eye of *M.A.S.H.* producers and was offered her first United States acting job as a Vietnamese refugee in the popular TV show set in the Korean War of the early 1950s.

Some time later, Kieu was chosen by Amy Tan to star in *The Joy Luck Club*, a film based on Tan's best-selling novel. Kieu's past experiences would prove valuable in cre-

ating the role of Suyuan, displaced mother of an accultur-
ated daughter.

"Art imitates life, life imitates art," Kieu told CCSN
students in an event sponsored by Student Government.

The Joy Luck Club opened many doors for the actress,
and she continued acting, becoming a consultant on Vietnamese film and TV scenes. Being a humanitarian, she
founded the Vietnamese Children's Fund, which has built
12 schools and helped many children in Vietnam.

With all that has happened to her, Kieu has gained
much wisdom. She offered this positive advice to anyone
willing to listen: "Any dream can come true, but it is difficult. It is not the beauty of it, but the passion."

Viet Dinh: White House Attorney

Eric Lichtblau

In May 2001 Viet Dinh became the first Vietnamese American assistant attorney general of the United States. As Eric Lichtblau reports in the following selection, Viet Dinh's escape from Vietnam after the Communist North Vietnamese took over democratic South Vietnam deeply influenced his political philosophy, making him especially sensitive to the importance of applying the law equally to all people. Viet Dinh is often credited as the chief architect of the Patriot Act, which was passed in an effort to enhance national security after the September 11, 2001, terrorist attacks. He began his political career as a volunteer in a voter registration center while still in high school, and after completing his education at Harvard Law School, he became a legal clerk for Supreme Court Justice Sandra Day O'Connor. He served as assistant attorney general of the United States for legal policy from 2001 until 2003.

Eric Lichtblau is a reporter in the Washington bureau of the *New York Times.*

At age 34 [in 2002, Viet Dinh] already has filled a resume befitting a man twice his age: boat refugee from Vietnam, Oregon fruit picker, Orange County burger-flipper, Harvard Law School graduate, U.S. Supreme Court clerk, Georgetown Law School professor, constitutional scholar, lawyer to a high-powered congressional committee. His is "a spectacular American story," Sen. Pete V. Domenici (R-

Eric Lichtblau, "At Home in War on Terror; Viet Dinh Has Gone from Academe to a Key Behind-the-Scenes Role. Conservatives Love Him, Others Find His Views Constitutionally Suspect," *Los Angeles Times*, September 18, 2002, p. A1. Copyright © 2002 by Eric Lichtblau. Reproduced by permission.

N.M.) said in introducing Dinh to the Senate during his confirmation hearings 16 months ago.

Dinh's current role as an assistant attorney general clearly has given him his most important platform yet. At first a somewhat obscure player in [U.S. Attorney General John] Ashcroft's Justice Department, his prominence in recent months has made him both a darling of the conservative movement and a lightning rod for criticism from liberal-leaning politicians and civil rights activists who assert that his views run roughshod over the Constitution.

Architect of the USA Patriot Act

On topics as far-ranging as gun control, cyber pornography, human trafficking and the selection of new federal judges, Dinh has played an increasingly critical role in shaping federal law enforcement policy. But nowhere has his impact been felt more keenly than in the Bush administration's highest priority: its aggressive war on terrorism.

Dinh was the chief architect of the USA Patriot Act, the legislation approved by Congress in the wake of the Sept. 11 [2001] attacks that gives law enforcement agencies vastly expanded powers to track terror suspects. He has been the official responsible for crafting a series of antiterrorism initiatives that would, among other things, require the fingerprinting of potentially tens of thousands of visiting foreigners from Middle East countries and would put foreign students on a much tighter leash.

He revamped the law enforcement guidelines that Ashcroft announced in May [2002] to give FBI agents new powers to snoop in mosques and surf the Internet. And he is now working on a plan to promote better coordination within the Justice Department and with agencies such as the CIA, a task aimed at preventing the communication breakdowns that preceded Sept. 11.

"I did not sign up for a war," Dinh said in an interview.

"But it's a privilege, a profound honor really, to serve your country in a time of crisis. I can't imagine a better place for me to be right now.". . .

A Gold-Medal Level of Service

Dinh, a wiry, energetic man who spews out ideas and legal theory at a furious staccato clip, has turned his boss into one of his biggest fans. "It's hard to point to a part of this department," Ashcroft said in an interview, "that isn't related to sound legal policy, so [Dinh] has become an integral part of virtually every decision we make. . . . He operates on a gold-medal level."

Dinh recalls the instructions Ashcroft gave him when he took over the job [in 2001]. "He told me: 'The art of leadership is the redefinition of the possible. I want you to be the think tank to help me redefine the possible for the Department of Justice.' That was a great charge for an academic," Dinh said.

Some Republicans even speculate that Dinh could someday be a candidate for the first Asian American justice on the Supreme Court. . . .

A Courageous Escape

Nearly a quarter-century [after he escaped Vietnam], Dinh still becomes emotional when remembering one scene: his mother in a Malaysian port, wielding an ax that seemed bigger than she was, whacking holes in the side of the vessel so she and five of her children would not be sent back out to sea.

It was 1978. Dinh was 10. His father was being held as a political prisoner in the family's war-ravaged homeland, when his mother, Nga Thu Nguyen, tried to escape by sea with Viet and the other children. They were among 85 people crammed on a 15-foot-long boat, but as Dinh's mother recalled in a recent telephone interview from her

Garden Grove [California] home, "after three days, the boat was broken. After seven days, there was no more food or water."

After 12 days, she had lost nearly all hope. But they came upon a Thai fishing crew who gave them food and gas, helped fix the boat and pointed them toward land. They reached Malaysia—only to be met by gunshots from a patrol boat. The Malaysians didn't want them. Their boat managed to dock, but Nguyen realized that the port police would force them to leave the next morning, so she crept back out to the boat alone that night with an ax, she said. "I just hit it and hit it and made holes everywhere," she said.

Dinh, recounting the events [in 2001] before the Senate Judiciary Committee as his nomination was considered, said it demonstrated for him the "incredible courage" of his mother and the "incredible lengths" to which people will go in search of freedom.

The administration's critics now find it ironic that Dinh, a refugee himself and an inspiration to many Asian Americans in Southern California, would advance policies that civil libertarians say place many Arabs and Arab Americans under a cloud of suspicion. But Dinh counters that his experience has given him a "special sensitivity to what it means to be an American" and how important it is to apply the law equally, regardless of race or ethnicity.

After six months as refugees in Malaysia, Dinh's family made it to Oregon for Thanksgiving of 1978. They picked strawberries for menial wages, sending money back to Dinh's father and a sibling hiding out in Vietnam. After Mt. St. Helens erupted in 1980, the crop damage forced his family to relocate to Fullerton [California].

In Orange County, the teenager worked with his mother in a sewing shop and put in time at fast-food restaurants after school. The family's persistence paid off in 1983 when Dinh's father finally made it to America. Dinh's parents wanted him to be a doctor. But politics was his passion, an interest fueled by his mother.

"He had a hatred of the Communists because I made him understand it was the Communists who had taken his father away from the house and put him in prison," Nguyen said. "I instilled that in him early on."

Like many Vietnamese immigrants, Dinh's emotional experience in his homeland steered him toward the Republican Party because of the GOP's hard-line stance against communism.

Politically Astute

Garden Grove Councilman Van Tran remembers Dinh, just out of Fullerton High School, volunteering to work the phone banks at an Asian American voter registration center set up by then-Rep. Robert K. Dornan.

"He used to call me *anh*, or 'elder brother.' He stood out even then as a lanky 18-year-old because he was someone who was very quick and very witty," Tran said.

Dinh's reputation as affable, bright and politically astute would follow him through Harvard University and Harvard Law School, which he attended with the aid of scholarships and graduated magna cum laude, and to the U.S. Supreme Court, where he clerked for Justice Sandra Day O'Connor.

"He was a wonderful law clerk," O'Connor recalled recently. "I was so fascinated by his background and the fact that he had arrived on our shores with nothing but the clothes on his back, yet somehow he had persevered."

CHRONOLOGY

2879 B.C.

King Hung Vuong is the first ruler of the nation of Vietnam (known as the kingdom of Van Lang).

207

Chinese general Zhao Tuo rules Vietnam.

111

Vietnam becomes province of Chinese Empire.

A.D. 39

National heroines, the Trung sisters, lead a revolt to drive the Chinese out of Vietnam.

939

Vietnamese liberator General Ngo Quyen defeats Chinese military forces. Ten centuries of Chinese rule come to an end.

1615

The first Catholic mission in Vietnam is opened near the city of Danang by French Jesuits.

1858

The French military seizes control of Danang.

1887

The French declare a new colony, Indochina, made up of Vietnam, Laos, and Cambodia.

1930

Ho Chi Minh organizes the Indochinese Communist Party to oppose French rule.

1940–1945

Japanese troops occupy Indochina from September 1940 until August 1945. The French resume rule in August. Ho Chi Minh forms a guerrilla army called the Vietminh to fight French occupation.

1954

The Vietminh defeat the French at Dien Bien Phu. On July 20 Vietnam is divided along the seventeenth parallel to form a northern zone, under Communist leader Ho Chi Minh, and a southern democratic zone under Prime Minister Ngo Dinh Diem. North Vietnam declares itself an independent Communist nation. The United States, fearing an increase in Communist power in Southeast Asia, supports the South Vietnamese.

1955

Ngo Dinh Diem becomes president of South Vietnam (the Republic of Vietnam).

1964

The Gulf of Tonkin Resolution is passed. President Lyndon Johnson suspects North Vietnamese forces of sinking U.S. battleships in the Gulf of Tonkin and authorizes the bombing of North Vietnam. This marks the first official involvement of the United States in the Vietnam War.

1968

Communist forces launch the Tet Offensive, a series of surprise attacks against the South Vietnamese. The attacks mark a turning point in the Vietnam War.

1973

U.S. involvement in Vietnam officially ends after the Paris Peace Accords.

1975

On April 30 North Vietnamese Communist forces seize control of South Vietnam. The first wave of refugees, approximately 130,000, enters the United States. Congress passes the Indochina Migration and Refugee Assistance Act, which establishes programs for resettlement.

1976

The plight of the "boat people" garners international attention. Refugees leave Vietnam en masse in small, dilapidated boats hoping to find safe harbor. Tens of thousands of Vietnamese die while trying to escape.

1980

The Refugee Act of 1980 is passed, amending the official definition of a refugee and outlining procedures to assist displaced persons with resettlement. The Socialist Republic of Vietnam and the United Nations Commission for Refugees establish the Orderly Departure Program to facilitate refugee resettlement. In Vietnam, Communists expel ethnic Chinese.

1982

The Vietnam Veterans Memorial, designed by Maya Lin, is erected in Washington, D.C.

1988

The Amerasian Homecoming Act is passed, allowing the Vietnamese children of American fathers to emigrate from Vietnam.

1992

Vietnamese American journalist Andrew Lam wins the World Affairs Council's Excellence in International Journalism Award.

1996

Eugene Trinh, a physicist born in Saigon, raised in Paris, and educated in the United States, becomes the first Vietnamese American to travel into space on a NASA space-ship. Trinh served as a mission payload specialist on the space shuttle *Columbia*.

1999

Hundreds of protesters converge on a Westminster, California, video store after owner Truong Tran posts a picture of Ho Chi Minh and the flag of Communist Vietnam in his window.

2000

Three Vietnamese American athletes, Tawny Binh, Michelle Do, and Khoa Nguyen, compete for the U.S. table tennis team in the 2000 Summer Olympics. President Bill Clinton visits Vietnam.

2001

President George W. Bush names Vietnamese American law professor Viet Dinh assistant attorney general for the Office of Legal Policy.

2002

Daughter from Danang, a documentary about Vietnamese American Mai Thi Hiep and her reunion with her Vietnamese family, wins three prestigious film awards and is nominated for an Academy Award.

2005

In March, Zen master Thich Nhat Hanh visits Vietnam after years of exile. The controversial visit upsets many in the Vietnamese American community who oppose the Vietnamese Communist government.

FOR FURTHER RESEARCH

Vietnam

Rick Berg and John Carlos Rowe, eds., *The Vietnam War and American Culture*. New York: Columbia University Press, 1991.

David Chanoff and Doan Van Toai, *Portrait of the Enemy: Vietnam, a Portrait of Its People at War*. New York: I.B. Tauris, 1996.

Larry Engelmann, *Tears Before the Rain: An Oral History of the Fall of South Vietnam*. New York: Oxford University Press, 1990.

Stanley Karnow, *Vietnam: A History*. New York: Penguin, 1984.

Literary Classics of the United States, *Reporting Vietnam, Part Two: American Journalism, 1969–1975*. New York: Library of America, 1998.

Robert McKelvey, *The Dust of Life: America's Children Abandoned in Vietnam*. Seattle: University of Washington Press, 1999.

Olivia Skelton, *Vietnam: Still Struggling, Still Spirited*. New York: Marshall Cavendish, 1998.

Marilyn B. Young, *The Vietnam War Years, 1945–1990*. New York: HarperPerennial, 1991.

The Early Immigrants

Nathan Caplan, John K. Whitmore, and Marcella H. Choy, *The Boat People and Achievement in America: A Study of Family Life, Hard Work, and Cultural Values*. Ann Arbor: University of Michigan Press, 1992.

Mary Terrell Cargill and Jade Quang Huynh, *Voices of Vietnamese Boat People: Nineteen Narratives of Escape and Survival.* Jefferson, NC: McFarland, 2000.

Kim Ha, *Stormy Escape: A Vietnamese Woman's Account of Her 1980 Flight Through Cambodia to Thailand.* Jefferson, NC: McFarland, 1997.

David Haines, ed., *Cambodians, Laotians, and Vietnamese in America.* Totowa, NJ: Rowman & Littlefield, 1989.

Jade Ngoc Quang Huynh, *South Wind Changing.* St. Paul, MN: Graywolf, 1994.

Gail Paradise Kelly, *From Vietnam to America: A Chronicle of the Vietnamese Immigration to the United States.* Boulder, CO: Westview, 1977.

Darrel Montero, *Vietnamese Americans: Patterns of Resettlement and Socioeconomic Adaptation in the United States.* Boulder, CO: Westview, 1979.

Scott C.S. Stone and John E. McGowan, *Wrapped in the Wind's Shawl: Refugees of Southeast Asia and the Western World.* San Rafael, CA: Presidio, 1980.

Later Waves

Hien Duc Do, *The Vietnamese Americans.* Westport, CT: Greenwood, 1999.

Duong Van Mai Elliott, *The Sacred Willow: Four Generations in the Life of a Vietnamese Family.* New York: Oxford University Press, 1999.

James M. Freeman, *Hearts of Sorrow: Vietnamese-American Lives.* Stanford, CA: Stanford University Press, 1989.

Susan Gall, ed., *The Asian-American Almanac: A Reference Work on Asians in the United States.* Detroit: Gale Research, 1995.

Nazli Kibria, *Family Tightrope: The Changing Lives of*

Vietnamese Americans. Princeton, NJ: Princeton University Press, 1993.

Patrick Du Phuoc Long, with Laura Ricard, *The Dream Shattered: Vietnamese Gangs in America.* Boston: Northeastern University Press, 1996.

Qui Duc Nguyen, *Where the Ashes Are: The Odyssey of a Vietnamese Family.* Reading, MA: Addison-Wesley, 1994.

Andrew X. Pham, *Catfish and Mandala.* New York: Farrar, Straus and Giroux, 1999.

Paul James Rutledge, *The Vietnamese Experience in America.* Indianapolis: Indiana University Press, 1992.

Ronald Takaki, *Strangers from a Different Shore: A History of Asian Americans.* Boston: Little, Brown, 1989.

De Tran, Andrew Lam, and Hai Dai Nguyen, eds., *Once upon a Dream: The Vietnamese-American Experience.* Kansas City, MO: Andrews McMeel, 1995.

Helen Zia, *Asian American Dreams: The Emergence of an American People.* New York: Farrar, Straus and Giroux, 2000.

Web Sites

VIETgate, www.vietgate.net. This search engine and gate for Vietnamese content Web sites bills itself as the "Gateway to the Online Vietnamese Community."

Vietnamese Americans: Lessons in American History, www.tolerance.org/teach/web/vietnamese. Southern Poverty Law Center's tolerance.org Web project provides a collection of instructional materials dealing with Vietnamese American history.

Vietnamese in the United States, California State Library, www.library.ca.gov/assets/acrobat/vietnamese.pdf. This Web site, compiled by librarian Angie Nguyen, is a large, useful collection of brief articles and facts on subjects including population statistics, language, religion, customs, holidays, and popular authors.

Vietnamese Studies Internet Resources Center, www. vstudies.org. A collection of information about Vietnamese culture and history complied by Mark Pfeifer, director of the Hmong Resource Center at the Hmong Cultural Center, St. Paul, Minnesota.

Vietnam Globe, http://vietnamglobe.com. A news service subsidiary of World News Network that provides news and information on current affairs in Vietnam.

Westminster, California,
19–20, 99
*When Heaven and Earth
Changed Places*
(Hayslip), 152–55
Willman, Alys, 121
Wirick, Sang, 126–27, 129
women
  changing roles of, 83–86,
  88, 101, 106–11

education and, 146
  see also spouses, abuse of
Wurts, Jay, 153–54

Yellow Lotus (film),
157–58
YMCA, 59, 74
youth, 12–13, 21–22,
  80–82, 104, 110–13, 128
  see also children; gangs